Joe

A Life of Mischief, Humor, and Joy

LOVE JOE

Pamela —
I am grateful to share these stories of my brother with you! Be joyful and happy.
Thank you —
Sandra Bartel

10/8/06

Jamala,
Happy Birthday!
I hope that your birthday is the happiest — and that your dreams come true.
Be happy. I love you.
Grandma

A Life of Mischief, Humor, and Joy

Sandra Bartel

Sandbur Publishing
2018

Joe: A Life of Mischief, Humor, and Joy
2018 © Sandra Bartel

All rights reserved.

Printed in the United States of America
No part of this book may be used or reproduced in any manner whatsoever without written permission from the publisher except in the case of brief quotations embodied in critical articles and reviews.

ISBN: 978-0-692-07614-9

Edited by Connie Anderson, Words and Deeds, Inc.
Interior and Cover Design by Sue Stein, Dragonstone Press

Photos © Sandra Bartel
Photo page 109 courtesy Cortney Molling

Sandbur Publishing
La Crosse, Wisconsin

DEDICATION

In loving memory of our parents, Jim and Rita, for all the times you said, "I wish I had kept a book of stories about some of the things Joe has said and done."

TO: SANDRA AND PAUL —
THANK YOU FOR
EVERYTHING!
I LOVE YOU SO MUCH.
LOVE JOE

TABLE OF CONTENTS

Introduction   1

Chapter One
Birth to Age 4   3

Chapter Two
Early Childhood: Age 4–11; 1973–1980   7

Chapter Three
Teen Years: Age 12–21; 1981–1990   17

Chapter Four
Adult Years: Age 22–48; 1991–2017   25

Chapter Five
Stories of Joe: Out and About   43

Chapter Six
"Joe-isms"—Random Funny Comments and Stories   67

Chapter Seven
Mixed-up Words and Sentences   77

Chapter Eight
Telephone Joe   83

Chapter Nine
Misbehaving Joe   87

Chapter Ten
Inspirational Joe						91

Chapter Eleven
Peculiar Joe						97

Chapter Twelve
Tell It Like It Is, Joe					103

Chapter Thirteen
Joe's Jaunts						107

Closing Comments					113

INTRODUCTION

"He is the joy in my heart, and the pain in my ass."

That is how I have often described my brother, Joe. Born with Down syndrome, he is full of love and sweetness, sure, but it is his lifelong unintentional humor, mixed-up sentences, funny conversations, innocent adventures, goofy faces, spot-on imitations when describing what people look or sound like, and his unending rascally antics that led me to write this book.

A family friend described Joe as, "Special, because he's Joe, a young man completely guileless when dealing with others. He possesses a freedom to be himself and sometimes to ignore convention and act on impulse. Haven't many of us wished to act on a whim, or disregard being tactful at times?"

Yes, we have, but Joe, it seems, always takes it to the next level.

All anecdotes, Joe-isms, conversations, and adventures are stories of true events that were submitted over the years by family, friends, relatives, neighbors, teachers, and anyone else who has ever had the pleasure to experience an encounter with Joe.

This book is written with a deep respect for those who have raised or cared for an individual with Down syndrome. My hope is that their lives have been as profoundly enriched by their special person as I have been with Joe.

Joe has lived with my family, husband Paul, and children Bryan and Beth, since 1996, joining us when he was twenty-six. He has been a constant source of joy and laughter (and clearly, some frustrations). Just when we think we have seen or heard it all, he comes up with something new.

My hope is that I have captured and conveyed both the essence of his character through his wacky, playful, hilarious life experiences and adventures, and silly Joe-isms, in addition to his unique and charming personality.

It is with gratitude and appreciation to my family and friends for their encouragement that I share these stories.

CHAPTER 1

BIRTH TO AGE 4

Joseph was born just before Christmas 1969. Another baby in the household was no big deal as he was the tenth child in the family, preceded by eight older sisters and one brother. Another sister would be born five years later. I am the fourth oldest child in our family.

As an eleven-year old, I learned quickly that this baby was a big deal. I was giddy with excitement on Christmas Eve day when Dad gave me permission to go with him to bring my mom and baby brother home from the hospital. Dad and I walked hand in hand into the hospital, and as we took the elevator up to the fifth-floor maternity unit, he seemed preoccupied with thoughts other than the exciting fact that today was Christmas Eve—and we were here to take baby Joseph and Mom home.

As we approached the nurse's station near Mom's room, we were greeted by sad smiles and kind hellos from the staff. Our arrival at Mom's private hospital room interrupted a conversation she and the doctor were having. Baby Joseph was in the nursery. I skipped off to look out the window. Once the novelty of being five floors up off the ground wore off, I joined Mom and Dad as the doctor continued the discussion.

This was a happy day for me to be bringing another baby home—and to be the first of my siblings to see, touch, and kiss him. The conversation between the doctor and my parents continued. I was not included but knew enough to not interrupt. I heard words unfamiliar to me: Down syndrome, disabilities. What did those words mean, and what did they have to do with our family? Why did Mom have tears in her eyes and Dad look so sad? Then I heard the word "institution."

This was a time when children with varying disabilities, including those with Down syndrome, were sometimes institutionalized. I remember as my mom wiped away her tears, drew in a long breath, and with a stern look, she and my father told the doctor in no uncertain terms that there would be no institutions for Joe. "Absolutely not! He will be raised by us in this family, just like all his sisters and brother. He will walk. He will talk. He will go to school. He will be cared for and loved just as our other children."

Before the doctor left the room, he hugged my mom, shook my dad's hand, nodded, and said, "I have no doubt you will raise him as beautifully as your other children, and that Joseph will be a happy child in your home." Then Mom gave me a big smile, hugged me tightly, and suggested we get home to show everyone our new baby brother.

Years later our dad would describe his first reaction to learning that his son had Down syndrome like "…diving into a tank of ice water." He went on to say, "After that, it is life. I'm glad he was born into a large family and not as an only child." Meaning, I would guess, that by then he and my mom were seasoned parents, and there would be other kids to help with his care and supervision.

A day or so after coming home from the hospital, my mom put baby Joey, as we all called him, in the middle of our large dining table. All of us children hovered around him, checking him out. She explained that Joey was "special." She pointed out his unique features: his inward curved pinky fingers, flat feet, elongated tongue, upward-slanted eyes, and tiny ears. His weakened muscles would need special exercises; he was going to be slower to walk, talk, and to do the same things we did, she said. Most of all, we were to love this special baby because he would need all of us to help him to learn and grow. Oh, and one more thing she told us: "You will never, ever, tease anyone if they are retarded or be mean to others, telling them they are a 'retard'."

Two weeks after his birth, my parents went out for dinner and several of the older sisters babysat Joey. As we changed his diaper, his umbilical cord came off. We thought we had "broken" him. Frightened, we called the restaurant, asking specifically for our mom. We were too scared to talk to our dad for some reason, thinking he would be real mad at us. Through tears, one of us told mom what had happened, and that we think we "broke" the baby. She cried with laughter, promising to be home shortly. Minutes later she arrived home to comfort her frightened daughters. She explained how babies receive nourishment and oxygen in the womb through the mother, and after the baby is born, the umbilical cord is clamped and cut in a painless procedure. She showed us the dried-up stump, and how Joey's belly button would look like ours once it was healed. We were so relieved to know we had caused no harm to the baby.

According to our mom's notations in his baby book, Joe did indeed develop at a slower pace. He was ten months old before he could sit up straight by himself; his first real crawling wasn't until he was a full year old; and his first tooth didn't come in until he was fourteen months old. Generally, the first baby tooth comes in at about six months. Joe was a calm, happy baby. On his first birthday, like most other children, he put his fingers in the chocolate frosting on his cake and right into his mouth with a big smile as he discovered this new sweet flavor.

Joe was born at a good time in the late 1960s, just as programs for children with disabilities began to be developed. At age two, Joe attended an early childhood development school for children with developmental and physical disabilities. The primary focus was to develop Joe's large motor skills, to strengthen his muscles, and to work on his speech.

Whether it was to release frustration or to soothe himself, Joe would get into a crawling position on all fours. He would rock back and forth for minutes on end. Since he would intentionally bang his head on his crib or the wall while rocking, our mom fashioned a padded helmet of sorts to protect his head. When that wasn't enough, the physician ordered him to wear a helmet as needed for protection. He eventually grew out of rocking on all fours, and instead would rock in a more harmless seated position.

Joe captured my heart from the second I laid eyes on him, and even more so when I learned he had special needs. Everything about him touched my heart. I was intrigued by him because he was different from my other siblings when they were babies. I loved to help my mom with Joe's muscle-strengthening exercises. I helped to coax him to walk, speak, or hold a color crayon. I would read, talk, and sing to him until he wiggled and squiggled off my lap and crawled away on to something else that interested him. In a sense, I cared for Joe as though he was my own little human doll.

I was about thirteen years old when I very seriously told our mom that I would always take care of Joe. She would never have to worry about him because I would always be there for him, regardless. I cared for him deeply, and if he was smiling; then I was smiling.

CHAPTER 2

EARLY CHILDHOOD
AGE 4-11; 1973-1980

At age four, Joe attended Washburn School, a public school with a special education program. He had a dedicated staff of professionals working with him. It was good for him to have both the one-on-one instruction as well as the opportunity to interact and socialize with classmates with similar abilities.

About this time the ophthalmologist prescribed corrective lenses for Joe—and he was to begin wearing glasses. If our parents could foresee what was about to come, they would have invested in an optical store franchise. Never mind the fact that these corrective lenses would help Joe's vision, he did not like them one

Joe at Myrick Park, age 7, dirty and tired-looking.

bit. He threw his glasses. He broke his glasses. He hid his glasses. He stomped on his glasses. Our mom made an elastic strap to keep the glasses secured to Joe's face. However, despite her best efforts, Joe was still not a fan of having to wear them. He threw numerous pairs of glasses out of house and car windows, or he would simply break them by snapping the bows. Eventually he grew to accept the glasses and discontinued the battle of trying to get rid of them.

Joe was passionate about *Sesame Street* and all the characters on the show. Over the years, Santa Claus would bring him a stuffed Bert and Ernie, Big Bird, Cookie Monster, Kermit the Frog, and Grover. Grover became Joe's constant companion. He would sit for a long time looking at and talking to Grover. While watching hours of *Sesame Street*, Joe learned to talk in a voice like the show's characters. This should have served as a warning to my parents and others that Joe would become quite an actor himself. He imitated and impersonated television actors, *Sesame Street* and Muppet characters. He loved the attention he received with his spot-on imitations, and the way his silliness made others laugh. He was an entertainer.

Joe having fun running through
the sprinkler in 1977 at age 7½.

Early Childhood: Age Four to Eleven

Early on in his schooling, report cards and notes home to our parents began to include words such as "imp," "rambunctious," "inquisitive," "attention seeker," and "behavior is unpredictable."

Houdini Joe

Unpredictable behavior, indeed. It was not that Joe was being outwardly defiant. He simply did what he wanted to do at the time that it moved him. An early prognosis included that his physical development may be slow, and he might not be very active. Au contraire. He had to be watched constantly. When he was not, he was a slippery little bugger, an escape artist of sorts. He was so quiet he could put a cat burglar to shame.

An episode Dad recalled:

Joe was six-and-a-half years old. At five o'clock in the morning, still dark outside, Joe pushed out a screen in the front door. He climbed out and walked down the street. There was a drinking fountain on the corner one block away. He took a drink of water and walked another block south. Seeing a lighted doorbell on a house, he rang the doorbell and laid down on the front steps. The homeowners came to the door, found Joe laying down, still in his footed pajamas, and brought him into their home. They called the police and then started calling neighbors, hoping someone would know this little boy. One neighbor thought he might be Joe. At 5:30 a.m., they called our house and Mom and I went over to pick him up.

Joe liked the attention so much he performed the same act the following week. Two weeks later our family moved to a new neighborhood about a mile away. Unfortunately, the move did not deter Joe from escaping or exploring the neighborhood. In fact, it intensified.

As our new next-door neighbor, Alice, shared:

In September 1976, Jim and Rita and their family moved next door to us. I hated to see our old neighbors leave. Little did I realize that this fine family, and especially six-year-old Joey, would walk into my heart so soon.

Our daughter Amy was home from college for the weekend and came into our bedroom at 12:30 a.m., quite alarmed. "Mom, somebody's out in our back yard. I think it's Joey Burns!"

I looked out and she was right. Amy called Joey's parents, saying that I'd bring him to their front door. I went out into the yard, picked up Joey, who looked darling in his footed pajamas, and carried him next door. Joey leaned away from me, looked directly into my eyes and said, "I love you, Alice!"

Joe has said and done so many endearing things to all of us, but nothing will ever touch me like that first remark.

Shortly after those incidents, our parents had an identification bracelet made and secured it on Joey's wrist. His name, address, and phone number were imprinted on the bracelet. It came in handy multiple times over the years when he would slip out of the house undetected.

The front door was too heavy for Joe to open so the back door was his escape door of convenience. In an attempt to dissuade Joe from sneaking out of the house at all hours, at least a half dozen locks were strategically located on the door, each higher than the next—which just proved to be a challenge for Joe. He was creative in how he would stack chairs and add a booster seat for more height to get the locks open if he wanted to go out. He was so quiet. If one of the older kids walked down the stairs or across the room, you could hear the floor creaking. If one of us came in past curfew, the door would moan and groan. Mysteriously, Joe deftly avoided all the creaks and cracks and, heard by no one, he disappeared out of the house.

It was not unusual to get a very-early morning phone call from a neighbor up the street asking if it was okay that Joe was over and eating breakfast with them.

If he wasn't heading outside in the wee hours of the morning, then he would get up, turn on all the kitchen lights, open the refrigerator door wide, and turn on all the burners on the stove. Or, perhaps he would eat half of a cake that was left on the counter, and then go back to bed.

Early one morning one of the older sisters was outside in search of an escaped Joe. Half way down the block a college student was walking him home. The young man had come downstairs to find Joe in his living room, sitting on his couch eating the pizza from the night before, and watching a show on the student's television. It was the volume of the television that woke the student. He said it took a few minutes to try to figure out if he was in the right house, and when realizing that he was, what to do with this little boy? It would not be the first time Joe would visit the guys in that house, and when he did, they would promptly walk him back home.

Our parents went out for dinner nearly every Friday night for as long as I can remember. Joe was generally in the care of his older siblings, and occasionally a non-relative babysitter. This was the perfect storm: parents out for the evening, sitters not always wise to the ways of Joe, and Joe on center stage ready for any opportunity to explore the neighborhood.

Ten-year-old Joe and his five-year old sister were left with a sitter. The sitter called the restaurant, frantic. She told our mom that when she had let Joe play in the backyard, he had disappeared. She couldn't leave the other child to look for Joe. Mom went back to the table and told Dad and their dinner friends to continue with their salads, that she would be back before their main entrée arrived at the table. After driving up and down nearby streets, she decided to check out a route Dad and Joe often walked. She went into the neighborhood bar a quarter of a mile away. There was Joe, on the bartender's side of the bar, rinsing glasses. She brought Joe home and was back at the restaurant in time to eat her entrée with the others.

The neighborhood bar and its patrons came to know Joe well. The owner could tell right away when Joe had a new babysitter because he would sneak out of the house and make a beeline to the bar. He would welcome Joe and offer him a soda to drink while he made a few phone calls to ensure Joe would get home safe and sound. No one could blame the guy for wanting to have a little fun on his own at the bar.

There would be many more episodes of Joe sneaking out of the house at all hours of the day, particularly if our mom was either in the shower or doing laundry downstairs because she could not hear him leave with the water or machines running. By now the family knew his go-to destination spots and would go there to retrieve him. But mostly, it was the kindness of neighbors who would call our house and let us know where he was, or they would simply walk him home.

Young Mischievous Joe

It is plausible that Joe was mischievous all in his own right; however, it was his older siblings' encouragement that really set Joe on the path to the whimsical side of life. On Friday nights, with our parents out for dinner, we'd play "dress up from the hamper." To the delight of his older siblings, Joe was a willing participant. He would be in his blue one-piece zip-up footed pajamas, and we would stuff as many clothes into his pajamas as we could. Then we would roll him around on the floor. Or, we would dress him up as a bag lady, a little girl, or an animal. We loved it…and so did he.

With Mom and Dad out, and the younger of his older sisters watching him, Joe pretended to be his favorite television character, the Incredible Hulk. He would pose in a way to show his muscles, turn up the music, and make loud noises like the Hulk. He lifted the empty clothes hamper over his head, threw it down the stairs with a roar, and stomped down the steps. Initially the girls pretended to be frightened of him. Then in full Hulk destruction mode, he grabbed the kitchen curtains and attempted to rip them from the valance. Ripped curtains were going to be a tough one to explain to Mom when she got home. The girls put a stop to his convincing Hulk impersonation as he pulled cushions from the sofa. For Halloween when he was eleven, he was appropriately dressed as the Incredible Hulk.

Many years later, Joe went through an exceptionally bad period of disobedient behavior that I attributed to his constant watching of the *Incredible Hulk* movie. Fed up with his attempts at destroying anything in his path, I took the VHS cassette tape and pulled the movie film out and slammed it into the garbage, telling him that his disobedient behavior had to stop, and that there would be no more Hulk in this house. It resonated within him and he began to behave better, but, still to this day, when he has been behaving poorly, he will occasionally ask me not to throw away one of his movies.

Joe was a devoted fan of *The Dukes of Hazzard* television show. He loved everything about the show: Bo, Luke, and Daisy Duke, and Sheriff Roscoe P. Coltrane. However, the best part of the show was not a person. It was the orange Dodge Charger, dubbed the General Lee, with the number 01 painted in white and black on each side. Friday nights was, to Joe's childhood self, the most anticipated day of the week because *The Dukes* was on. In each episode the Duke boys would be chased by the bad guys. The General Lee would become airborne for what seemed like far too long to be believable, or they would crash into the side of a building, another car, or a bunch of garbage cans and send them flying. Bo and Luke were always fine, nary a scratch on them, nor on the General Lee.

Joe couldn't get enough of the exciting car chases and would plead with the driver of any car in which he was a passenger to jump their car like the Duke boys jumped the General Lee. He would try to convince the driver to "bump into that car, hop the curb, go faster." Several times he would put his foot on top of the driver's foot and press down on the accelerator, or he would grab the steering wheel and try to hit a parked car. Fortunately, at the time he didn't have the strength to succeed. Mind you, the mandatory seatbelt law did not go into effect in Wisconsin until 1987, long after Joe would pull these stunts.

With his interest in cars piqued, he found great delight in messing with cars. It did not matter whose car it was. If the car door was unlocked, it was fair game to Joe. The cars could be parked in a garage, on the street, or in a parking lot. He would sneak up to the car, turn both the windshield and turn signals to "on," pop open the hood, and turn the radio to full blast. He would patiently stand by the car until the driver put the key in the ignition. He would erupt in laughter as the wipers flapped full tilt and the radio blared. To this day, he continues to mess with the windshield wipers on my car.

With Joe sitting just inches from the television, attentively watching his beloved *Dukes of Hazzard* half-hour show, it generally meant time that Joe didn't have to be watched so intensely because he rarely looked away from the television. An older sister learned otherwise. She was caring for Joe when she went out to the back yard, leaving Joe in front of the television. Apparently, Joe got bored with *The Dukes* and locked himself in the upstairs bathroom. Not only did he flush most of a roll of toilet paper, he also had taken the screen off the window and began tossing a full box of tissues out the window, one by one. Tissues floated to the ground like autumn leaves from a tree.

He went through a long stage of tossing things out the windows, and not just tissues. Our two-story home was built in the mid-1920s. The windows were interchangeable with the season, screens for warmer months and storm windows for the colder months. If desired, the storm windows could be opened and latched in place with about a four- or five-inch opening. It was the perfect amount of space necessary for all the items Joe felt the urge to toss out of the window.

Usually it was assorted stuffed animals, shoes, costume jewelry, a transistor radio, art supplies, or other smaller objects. However, one day, Joe decided to toss something different. He came across a basket of clean, freshly folded laundry, and promptly tossed it all out the front bedroom window. The basket contained all his sisters' lingerie. There it was, our bras, undies, nylons, and socks dangling from the large spruce tree in the front of the house for all the world to see. Many times, after the snow melted in the spring, we would find other treasures that had been tossed out the window months earlier.

A handful of times Joe would blow out the pilot light on the furnace in our parent's home, which would make the house smell like there was a gas leak, just to see the police and fire trucks arrive with lights on and sirens blaring. Fortunately, after a scolding by a police officer and a fireman that behavior stopped.

Whether at home or at school, Joe has always had a fascination with basements, furnaces, boiler rooms, and other mechanical equipment. Joe stayed with Paul and me for the weekend and thinking our basement would be a safe space for him to play by himself, we sent him down to play with the toys. Within minutes, all the lights, television, and electrical appliances went off. Joe had switched off all the circuit breakers one by one.

Joe had no fear. Not of the four lanes of traffic or the railroad tracks he had to cross to get to the neighborhood bar, or of walking into a stranger's house or garage, or of messing with electrical or mechanical equipment. He was so full of mischief he simply could not be trusted to be left alone.

CHAPTER 3

TEEN YEARS
AGE 12-21; 1981-1990

School Stories

Joe attended Lincoln Middle School from age twelve to eighteen. He and his classmates were engaged in learning educational skills such as reading, writing, basic math, art and music, as well as a variety of other programs designed to teach them every-day living and social skills.

Regardless of which school Joe attended, it was his quirky mission to investigate every room in the school until he located the boiler room. He was fascinated with the boiler and mechanical rooms, the janitor's room, the tornado shelter areas, and any other room in the school—except for the classroom.

A teacher reported that the first day she was teaching at Lincoln Middle School, Joe asked to go to the bathroom. When he didn't return to class after ten minutes, she went looking for him. She found him perched on top of the stall, hands holding his chin. Apparently, he looked like a gargoyle with incredible balance. As she expressed her frustration with him and concern for his safety, his only response to her was, "Surprise, surprise!"

By those words, I am guessing that he unwittingly meant, "Surprise, surprise, you have no idea how hard it is going to be for you to have me in your class."

In 1988, twenty students with special needs transferred from the middle school to a public high school. Joe was eighteen years old. This was the first group of students to join the high school, and it added a whole new dimension to the student body. These young students were known as Trainable Mentally Retarded (a term no longer used in today's society). Each student had his or her own unique personality and talents. Their day consisted of practicing domestic living skills, vocational skills, community life, art, music, and special therapy. These special students were an integral part of the high school and provided the best possible education for all the students, and most of them had never been around a peer with special needs.

For Joe the different school opened a whole exciting world to explore with new teachers who had no idea the challenges they would be presented, compliments of Joe and his unruly antics.

A teacher shared this story:
When we made the move to Central High School, we really wanted the move to go smoothly (Joe had no idea where the boiler room was!). One Friday afternoon, Steve, the guidance counselor, came to me and said, "Ah, I think maybe I should tell you about this one." I think I must have known it concerned Joe because I immediately said, "JOE!" Steve asked if he was a young man with Down syndrome who is short and kind of round. Yes, I told him. Steve said, "Well, he is standing in the boy's bathroom stark naked." Steve had asked Joe what he was doing, and Joe said he was getting ready to go swimming. When asked why he didn't get dressed in the pool locker room, Joe very calmly looked up at Steve and said, "Are you nuts?"

A family friend shared:
I can remember a time when Joe was about eighteen, and I met him at the

local grocery store with others from his class, doing some shopping. Joe greeted me politely. About five minutes later I met him with a six-pack of cola, being marched down the aisle by his teacher, no doubt because soda was not on the grocery list. I had to give him credit for trying to pull a fast one and slip something extra into the shopping cart.

Football Joe

My poor mom, thinking she was getting a much-needed break from Joe for a couple of hours, would frequently send Joe, a young teenager, with my dad to the high school football games. For whatever reason, my dad, who had a very tight bond with Joe and was a very responsible man in all areas of his life, just was not attentive to Joe at these football games. One night, Joe visited the broadcast booth and, like E.T., phoned home to chat with Mom. Mom coaxed Joe to let her talk with one of the men in the booth, interrupting them from their broadcasting duties. She asked the man to announce on the speaker during a break to have my dad come to the booth to collect Joe, which they did. Seconds later, my dad took the walk of shame to the broadcast booth to collect his runaway son.

At another game, Dad and a friend were talking, likely about golf. At the same time, Joe was engaged in serious conversation—on the field, in the middle of the huddle. The football players lost all concentration on the game as they chatted and laughed about Joe joining them in the huddle. Finally, he was escorted to the sidelines by the security personnel and returned to Dad.

Frequently bored with sitting in the stands watching the football game, Joe would slip away unnoticed by Dad. One such evening, he went out to the parking lot where he pulled and turned enough knobs to have the car owners wondering why their wipers started or why their radio was at full blast when the key was turned, and the car started. A few cars also had their hoods popped open. Joe went from car to car until my dad spotted him and ran down the stadium stairs to catch the teenage imp.

Seeing as how Joe had no interest in sitting still for even a few minutes to watch a football game with Dad, it was a bit of a surprise when he became one of the high school football team managers. The high school athletics department was very good about inviting some of those in the special education classroom to assist as managers for some of the sports teams, such as basketball and football. Having the individuals with varying abilities from the special education class as a manager was beneficial for everyone involved: Joe and his peers, the young football players who may not have ever had an interaction with an individual with a disability, and the coaching staff who were so good about encouraging the players to interact with these managers.

Back in the day, a football manager's responsibilities were to make sure the equipment was ready, keep the water bottles filled, and assist with whatever tasks the coaches requested of them. I don't know what Joe's assignments were, but it is highly likely that Joe didn't perform too many of those tasks.

The players really enjoyed and looked out for the managers. Well, they looked out for Joe as best as they could.

The practice field was behind the high school, and right next to an active railroad track. The field had chain link fencing around it with one section about four-feet high and the other section about eight-feet high. Joe loved trains. Any time a train went by at football practice, no matter what he was doing, he would stop and watch.

One day practice was about to start on the upper field. Two trains were on the tracks—one heading north, the other heading south. The northbound train was stopped. There was only one track, so it had to wait for its turn to proceed. Joe heard the locomotive approaching, dropped what he was doing, and took off running across the field, stopping at the fence at the far end of the field, near the railroad tracks. Joe was watching and watching, and finally, the one train had passed by.

Now it was the northbound train's turn to continue down the tracks. When Joe walked along the fence line, the coaches halted practice and focused on Joe. Then it happened. Joe scampered up and over the eight-foot chain link fence, tumbling down the last few feet into the knee-high weeds and grass. Back up on his feet again, he took off running down the tracks after the train, which was gradually picking up speed. Coach K, the quickest of the three coaches, chased after Joe as fast as he could, leaping over the four-foot-high second fence. Coach K grabbed the back of Joe's collar when he was about five feet from the caboose. Ouch! Coach felt a sharp prick as he grasped Joe's wrist to lead him back toward the field. Joe had well over two hundred sandburs on him, covering his face, hands, clothing, and shoes, from his leap into the tall weeds.

No matter where the football team played a game, but always the out-of-town games, Joe would seek out and climb up to the press box while the team was warming up on the field. It didn't take long to realize that one of the coaches needed to be on "Joe duty," keeping an eye on his whereabouts. However, at one such out-of-town game, Joe slipped out of sight and no one could find him. The coaches asked Becky, the team's athletic trainer, to help in the search for Joe. After several minutes, Becky found him. He had climbed up and into the press box booth and was chatting with one of the men who takes care of the scoreboard. Joe did not want to leave, but she did eventually coax him to come with her back to the field.

At another stadium, the press box was sixteen to twenty feet straight up in the air. Joe climbed it effortlessly, but once up there, he didn't know how to get down. None of the coaching staff could cajole him into coming down. Only Becky could sweet-talk him into coming down to safe ground. Though even she was tested to the limit at one stadium where Joe climbed precariously up and on top of a very high and very small press box roof. Urged on by the coaches, Becky raced to the press box where it took her fifteen minutes to very carefully get him off the rooftop.

It was Joe's second year as a football manager. On the first day of practice, Coach K parked his brand-new shiny car, one he had special ordered and had to wait for its arrival at the car dealership. Finding just the perfect, most safe spot, he parked it in front of the door that only the janitor of the high school used. Coach K proceeded on to the football field where the team was warming up for practice.

Joe, instead of using the exit doors nearest the locker room like all the other football players, decided to exit the school on his way to the practice field through the door supposedly used only by the janitors. For no good reason, Joe climbed onto the hood of Coach K's two-hour-old car, fresh off the dealership's lot. You know, the one that was parked in the most-safe spot. No, Joe did not simply climb on the hood of the car, he jumped up and down several times. Next, he climbed on to the top and jumped several more times. From there, he jumped on to the trunk, jumping some more. When the players yelled for Coach K, he ran up to his car to find three dents the size of a dinner plate—one on the hood, one on the top, and one on the trunk. The other coaches could not keep from laughing, but my dad didn't think the thousand dollars in damage was too funny.

Coach D, a dear favorite of Joe's, was the defensive coach. At practices and during games, when he paid attention to what he was supposed to be doing, Joe would stand next to Coach D. Midseason, during a game, Coach was giving signals to the sideline coaches. Lo and behold, there was Joe, copying each of Coach's signals. This went on for the next few games. Each time Coach D gave a signal, Joe would do the same signal.

Prior to the start of the last game of the season, Coach D told head coach, Coach K, that in the last quarter of the game, he would tell the team captain he would not be calling the plays, Joe would give the signals. It was fourth quarter on a cool autumn night. Joe was ready, standing there right next to Coach D, in his winter clothing and Irish tweed cap with the ear flaps down and covering his ears. Coach D would look at Joe, do the signal and verbally tell Joe the play. Then, for sixteen to twenty plays, Joe would turn to the players and correctly signaled each of the plays. At the end of the game all the players came off the field and together with the coaches hugged and congratulated Joe—none prouder than Coach D. Still today, whenever Coach D and Joe see each other, they give each other a big bear hug, and likely remember the good old football days of Joe's youth.

Joe was the high school football team manager for two years and at age twenty, the Central High School athletic department awarded Joe a varsity letter for his role on the team for the 1990 football season.

Chapter 4

ADULT YEARS
AGE 22-48; 1991-2017

Joe graduated from high school at age 21 and began to work at what was then called a sheltered workshop. They provide support for individuals with disabilities, including community and work-center employment. In the production plant he does a variety of tasks in a small group setting with a job coach. For local businesses, he may stuff envelopes, sort hangers into various sizes, sort screws and bolts, or similar piecemeal work. The other part of his work is what is called Day Services, where they teach every-day living skills, including cooking class, which he loves because they get to eat what they make.

When Joe first began to work there, a bus carrying an aide would come to our parents' home to both pick him up and then bring him home. Generally, his behavior on the bus warranted the bus aide to sit next to him simply to keep him seated while the bus was moving.

Our mom died in June 1995, when Joe was 25. For three years, Joe continued to live with our dad during the week and stayed with Paul and me and our two children, Bryan and Beth, ages thirteen and twelve, respectively, every Thursday, Friday, and Saturday. We brought Joe home to Dad on Sunday afternoons. This allowed Dad to have a break from caregiving and the opportunity to play a couple rounds of golf without having to worry about Joe. By July 1998, Joe was living with us permanently. With Dad's health beginning to decline, he asked Paul and me if we would consider becoming Joe's guardians. On July 14, 1999, Dad, Joe, Paul and I and the kids, went to court where the judge granted us legal guardianship of Joe. Dad died nine years later in March 2008.

Joe continued to work at the production plant, getting there on the bus that also carried others with disabilities, instead now picking Joe up at our house and transporting him to our home after work. With frequent complaints of Joe's bad behavior from his bus drivers, he eventually got kicked off the bus, permanently. Another man, who Joe did not get along with at all, was calling one of the female rider's names, such as "fat." Joe defended the girl and punched the guy. That was the final straw, and Joe was never to ride that bus again.

He has since been riding with a transportation company that picks him up for work in the morning in their car and brings him home in the afternoon. He continues to have issues with the very kind woman driver who very patiently puts up with him and his not-so-kind or grumpy behavior. When he doesn't behave appropriately, I fully support her when she assigns him to sit in the back seat for the next few days. He really wants to sit in the front seat, so it is generally an effective consequence for him.

However, one day while at work, I received a call from Joe's morning driver who was upset with Joe's foul mouth and behavior (he was giving the middle finger to people at traffic lights, including police). That evening I told Joe he would have to sit in the back seat for the next two days and not get to listen to his favorite radio station in the car. Simply put, he was not having any of it and said, "I not sit in the back seat. You can strap me onto the hood." Believe me, I am sure his driver would have loved to strap him on the hood.

Sweet or Sour Joe

Joe has two very distinct sides—Sweet or Sour—and there is not a lot of "in between." Joe's temperament and behavioral patterns are cyclical. When he is in the downswing, he is belligerent, negative, noncompliant, and difficult to redirect. More often than not, it is his mouth and a few unusual behaviors that get him in trouble. When Joe is in the upswing, he is helpful, sweet, happy, very funny, and loving. Those Sweet-Joe days are the days I really want to bottle.

While you never know what you are going to get from day to day, it is very apparent if he is Sweet or Sour Joe.

Sour Joe

Joe is affectionate with his words, hugs, and kisses. Or, quite the opposite, as was the case when Paul, my boyfriend (future husband), met nine-year-old Joe for the first time. Paul greeted him with a big smile and asked how he was. Joe retorted, "F*** you, A******." He learned this phrase as a four-year-old boy. The minute that he learned it was not acceptable language, it would never leave his vocabulary no matter what. Few people could ever get away with saying or doing some of the things that Joe has.

There have been many cringe-worthy moments when he has been more than willing to say what is on his mind or to point out the obvious. He will freely tell others to watch their language or keep their hands in their own space; however, he does not heed his own advice.

A teacher shared:

I will never forget my first year of teaching. All the administrators had their offices on the third floor. We had our classroom on the first floor. This meant the administrators could peek in or stop to visit anytime during the day, which they often did. This can be very nerve wracking for a first-year teacher. One day the director of personnel, along with a few colleagues, stopped in to visit. The director went around to all the

Joe's graduation, June 1991.

students asking their names and saying hello to each. Needless to say, Joe was in my class at the time. When the director came to Joe, he said, 'And who do we have here?' Before Joe opened his mouth, I knew. It was in his eyes. Joe looked up and promptly rattled off, very clearly, a long, long list of extremely colorful words. I was in shock. The director was in shock. I think everyone in the room, other than Joe, was in shock. Fortunately, the director had a great sense of humor. I cannot remember what he said to Joe, but I know he left the room laughing.

Decades later I was involved in a leadership program with area professionals, and this same man who Joe spouted off to was the coordinator of the leadership program. During a break we had a conversation in which I said, "You may or may not remember my brother. He was a student at Washburn Elementary when you were the administrator there. My brother was in the special needs program and has Down syndrome." Without hesitation this six-foot-seven hulk of a man, with hands the size of a grizzly bear, threw his hands up and bellowed, "I will never forget him—Joey Burns! He nearly dropped me to my knees with his greeting the day I first met him, when I had all the other school officials along."

From our parish priest at the time:
During Lent the pastors all concelebrated at a Mass for the special education students, of which Joe was a member. The late Father Jim was the principal celebrant and always gave the homily. Right in the middle of his homily one

year, Joe put up his hand and Father asked him what he wanted. Joe asked, 'Why are you so fat?' Needless to say, everyone burst out laughing, including Father Jim, and his homily stopped dead in its tracks. While I, along with the other pastors, came into the sacristy after Mass, I engendered further laughter by asking, 'Whoever said that Joey Burns was handicapped?'

As a teen, when Joe and Dad were walking, Joe fell on the ice. Dad said, "Oh, Joe, you fell on your buns."
Joe responded, "No, I fall on my ass. Get it right."

Joe and our parents visited a sister and her husband in Colorado. Out for dinner, the brother-in-law took Joe to the men's room. On their way out of the bathroom, Joe pinched a young adult blond man on the rear and said, "Hi Sweetie." The guy turned around, the brother-in-law stepped back, raising both hands, and said, "It's okay," and pointed to Joe. All was forgiven. How could you not? It's Joe!

While visiting two of our sisters in California, Joe rode in a car with one sister, and I was in the next car with the other sister. As they drove down the California I-405 freeway, Joe rode with his hand out the window, middle finger extended high in the air—for twenty-two miles. The sister he was riding with had no idea he was giving the one-finger salute for miles down the highway until we reached our destination. Once we told her what Joe had done, it all made sense. She now understood the quizzical looks and nasty glares from people as they passed her car on the freeway.

I took Joe along to my exercise class. To the plump woman exercising next to me, Joe said, "You eat too many cookies." When I admonished him and apologized to her, he said, "Well, she is fat!" The woman simply laughed and agreed and went back to her exercises.

Joe was holding the door open for his co-workers and others entering the production workshop where he works. An obviously overweight woman was entering with her adult son who also works there. Joe held the door open and to the woman said, "Get your fat ass in there."

She stopped, looked him in the eyes and said, "I work with your sister Sandra, and she would not like to know you are talking like that."

Joe straightened right up and said, "Oh, of course, now go on in and have a nice day!"

It was a beautiful, sunny day. Joe and his friend were sent outside to take a walk. Joe was not particularly happy about it. To show his dissatisfaction for having to take a walk, he walked with his right hand held high up in the air and his middle finger fully extended for the duration of his half-hour walk. Since then, the neighbors have been forewarned not to take it personally if they hear or see him doing that again.

On the evening of National Siblings Day, as I told him it was time for him to go to bed, he replied, "Kiss my ass." Clearly, Joe was so over celebrating Siblings Day.

Most mornings as he gets ready for work, Joe repeatedly calls me a F***erFace. It is never to my face. He is usually either in his bathroom or bedroom, and he says it softly, but loud enough so I can hear it. Normally I ignore it. One day in particular, I had had it and did not ignore it. I told him he was not allowed to have dessert that evening. When I got home from work he tried to butter me up with sweetness, followed me around the house, and asked, "You like suckers, do you?"

"No, I do not like suckers," I would reply.

"Yes, you do, you like s-u-c-k-e-r-s," spelling it out. He was doing anything he could to find a way to use words that rhyme with the swear word he had called me that morning. It was a long night of him getting the "u-c-k-e-r" out of his system.

Sometimes I must give him credit for the creative ways in which he swears. I have been contacted at work on several occasions because Joe was upsetting his fellow coworkers by using sign language to spell out the F word and other inappropriate words.

Many times, when the transportation service picks Joe up in the morning to take him to work, as we drive down the highway side by side, he will wave to me, and with a smile wide across his face he will mouth the words "F*** you" to me. I am certain the driver has no idea what he is saying. For all they know, he is simply smiling and waving to me.

Joe understands his swear words and finger business upset others, but in the heat of the moment he cannot control his impulsive self. He is so aware, in fact, he frequently will tattle on himself.

He had been watching *Cops* on the television downstairs and came upstairs to tell me the bad boy was swearing to the cops. "Want me to say those naughty words to you? That's what I do downstairs, you know."

A female coworker was upset with Joe and hit him on the back. Staff intervened and moved her to another work station. I asked what he did after she hit him. "I shoot my mouth off. Bigtime F words. I told her: 'skit, scat, scoot, scram, skedaddle, vamoose, get the hell out of here, go bug someone else.'" Who else can possibly get away with talking like that to their coworker?

After having been scolded for giving the finger to the garage door (yes, the garage door), Joe then scolded himself and said, "No finger business. Cross my heart and hope to live." Frankly, it is amazing he has lived this many years with his swear words and middle-finger business.

Most of the time I do what I can to ignore his foul language or middle finger. I understand it is how he releases frustration. I do not take it personally, and rarely does he say it directly to me. Typically, I ignore it. Other days, not so much—and I withhold his dessert at dinnertime as a consequence to his ill-behavior.

For example, in his typical fashion of starting his day by repeating over and over, "Sandra is a F***erFace," even before getting out of bed, I told him no dessert for supper. That evening, whether we wanted it or not, Paul and I had dessert. We did so intentionally to make him think about his behavior and how it affects him. He watched us eat our dessert, and with dejection in his voice he said to himself, "Sticks and stones will bust your bones and nasty words will never help you. And say nice kind things to your sister."

He would—*if he just had some impulse control.*

Sweet Joe

Sweet Joe is extremely soft and gentle when around babies and small children. He loves to cuddle and kiss the foreheads of babies or pick up and hug a toddler. From a very early age he was taught good manners that would put other children to shame. He was polite and welcoming, and expected the same of others. It came natural to Joe to have open arms ready to accept or to give a hug. In Joe's case, God gave you two cheeks; therefore, both were meant to be kissed.

As he grew into adulthood, he picked up some cool, smooth moves, learning how to turn on his charm to impress the ladies, and even a few men along the way.

When Joe and I are out and about running errands, getting his hair cut, or dining at a restaurant, for example, before we get out of the car I must remind him not to hug or kiss anyone; just offer them a handshake. Generally, I have wasted my breath because those instructions are completely lost on Joe. He cannot resist giving the grocer, doctor, cashier, or wait staff a hug, kiss, or back-of-the-hand kisses. It is Joe's special brand of love. His instant reward is their immediate reaction of delight.

He is an uncontrollable flirt. He is quick to tell a teenager how cute she is, or to the women how beautiful they are. "You look beautiful, you look," he will say. To the men it is, "You look handsome!" Even the not-soattractive person in the room is told how nice he or she looks. What an ego booster. How can you not be smitten with such a charmer?

Joe was helping me in the kitchen. I told him, "You are Mr. Wonderful, Joe Burns."

He thought about that for a couple of minutes; then replied, "Mr. Wonderful, huh? What you, Mrs. Perfect?"

Any time one of the men drivers pick Joe up for work he is super happy. He prefers the men over the women who pick him up most days. On this day, Big John arrived to take Joe to work. I left at the same time in my vehicle. Once the highway became two lanes, I drove side-by-side next to Big John's car. Joe was super excited. He waved like a beauty queen and excitedly pointed to John. Further down the road we were side-by-side at the traffic lights. Joe and I rolled down our windows. He had a huge smile and said, "Big John is here! Do you see him? Say hi! I FIND Big John!" I obliged and said hello to Big John. The lights changed and around the corner they went. John really could not know how happy he made Joe simply by picking him up for work. I smiled the rest of the way to work.

Joe was watching *The Muppets* movie. I called him up for bed. Instead of hearing him swear at me, I heard him say to the Muppets: "Goodnight. I will be back. See you on Wednesday night. I love you." I wish I were a Muppet!

Sometimes when one would least expect it, Joe's very deep-seated nurturing, emotional side shows. He possesses a profound sensitivity toward those who are hurting emotionally.

When we needed to put our family dog of nearly fifteen years to sleep, our daughter, Beth, came home from college. Beth, Joe, and I took the dog to one of our sister's home out in the country where a veterinarian would come to administer the euthanasia to our dog. We laid down Beth's favorite bedsheet on the backyard patio and sat down with the dog snuggled into

Beth's lap. With tears welling in all our eyes, Joe very quietly got up, moving to sit next to Beth and stroked her hair as he rubbed her back. He gently told her to stop crying and wiped a tear from her cheek. It was such a touching gesture.

He has always loved to go to funerals. He likes to observe the deceased person in the casket. I have witnessed so many times the gentle way he hugs the grieving family as if to say, I understand and want you to know that you'll be fine. It is often followed by him saying something silly which lightens the mood and brings an instant smile to those who need it most at that moment.

Every night he turns down Paul's and my bed, carefully folds the covers over, props up the pillows, and turns the light on next to the bed. Then, making a sweeping motion with his hand over the bed he asks, "Well, what you think?" Naturally, I make a grand show of appreciation and admit how beautiful the bed looks. As he hugs me goodnight, he insists that I "get home early after work" the next day. Regardless of what time I get home from work, when I step into the house, Joe greets me with a hug and a hearty "Welcome back!"

Enroute to Minneapolis, Joe and I were listening to and singing songs on my iPod. Joe started crying. I asked him why he was crying, and he said, "I am a good singer, you know." Then he wiped his eyes and started singing again like nothing had just happened. It was so sweet that he was so emotional over his own singing.

As children, every night at bedtime Mom would say, "Good night, Little Angels." In unison, we would all reply, "Good night, Big Angel." At Mom's funeral, with Dad and her children standing around her casket as it was being closed, we were all fighting tears. Joe simply spoke from his blessed heart, and said, "Good night, Big Angel." We all giggled in relief for the levity in the seriousness of this moment. Sometimes he gets it just right.

Gorilla Joe

Twelve-year-old Joe dressed up as a gorilla for Halloween. He had a brand-new gorilla facemask made of molded plastic with eyeholes and a narrow opening for the toothy smiling mouth. Black curly hair was stitched to the mask framing the face and sides of the face. A narrow band of elastic secured the mask to his face.

More than thirty years later, this gorilla mask is Joe's most prized possession from his childhood, now kept safe in a desk drawer. The eyes and one of the jawlines are cracking, showing signs of its age and wear. The elastic band has lost its elasticity and has a rubber band attached so it can still be worn.

Joe in his beloved gorilla mask.

Young Joe could wear his glasses behind the mask; older Joe will often wear his glasses on the outside or not at all. Gorilla Joe will not so sneakily enter the room or come up from behind and tap someone on the shoulder. Sometimes he speaks, other times he is silent. But the reaction is generally the same from those who are "scared" of the gorilla. We generate screams of fright or run from the room trying to get away from the gorilla. It is then that the mask is removed, and Joe calms us down by giving a hug and reassurance that, "It is me, I not really a gorilla. See, it is me, Joe Burns."

Gorilla Joe continues to make appearances throughout the year, not just the Halloween season. He has been known to wake up sleeping family or guests, show up at a teenage niece's birthday party, or appear at other random times.

Once when I was showering I thought I heard Joe in the room, but

Gorilla Joe scaring Beth.

when I glanced out I didn't see him. Then, with towel wrapped around me, I opened the shower curtain to find Gorilla Joe on the floor. He was on his belly, creeping like an alligator. I did the obligatory scream, calling, "Joe, come here quick! There's a gorilla in the bathroom. Hurry, come here, Joe."

Then for the next five minutes he continued to "scare" me behind the closed door. When I came out of the bathroom, he took off the mask and said, "It is me. I am your brother Joe!"

Another time Gorilla Joe came to the kitchen to scare me. A few minutes later he put the mask away and went into our bedroom to watch TV. Paul was in there and said to Joe, "Aaaahhh, you scared me with your mask on."

Joe, with no mask on, responded, "Nice try, Paul. That's my skin you're talking to."

The night before Halloween in 2014, in no uncertain terms, Joe told me, "I am going to work with my gorilla mask and I SCARE everyone." But he wouldn't be going to work the next day because he had a doctor appointment. Paul dropped us off at the clinic while he ran an errand.

Gorilla Joe insisted on bringing the mask in with him. I didn't bother to deny him. Hey, it was Halloween! So, in we go, mask on as we check in at the reception desk. Mask on as the nurse calls him to go back to the room, "scaring" all the women at the nurse's station. Mask on when the doctor walks into the room. The doctor couldn't stop laughing. It was not his regular doctor, so he was very unfamiliar with Joe, but he loved it.

After the appointment we humored Joe by taking him to his work to scare his coworkers with his gorilla mask since his heart was so set on it. Oh, the joy! I went in to his work with him. He wore the mask in and scared everyone. One of his job coaches acted perfectly scared and walked away from him in fright with Gorilla Joe following her. Finally, he lifted the mask, "It is ME! Joe Burns! It is me! I not a gorilla. It is a mask. See?"

Joe, the Grocery Store Cart Runner

Do not take Joe shopping at a grocery store, department store, or any other store where there are shopping carts and think that you will be the one to push the cart. That is Joe's self-appointed job. And it does not matter if you are there to buy one item or a cartful, he is going to man the shopping cart. Aside from clipping the heels of anyone in his path, Joe enjoys the fact that he is being helpful and involved in the shopping expedition. Pushing the cart also helps Joe to keep pace with those with whom he is shopping.

Since 1991, Joe has worked for an organization which offers supported employment, a production plant, and day services for individuals with disabilities. I did not feel the organization put enough effort into finding Joe suitable employment either within the production plant, or in the community where his skills and ability would benefit both the employer and Joe—where Joe could be challenged and successful amid the general public in our thriving community.

Dinner table conversation often focused on Joe's deplorable behavior at the production plant. The more attention he got for his negative attitude and poor behavior on the job, the worse he became. Frustrated, and with the realization that it was going to be up to us to find Joe a job in the community, we shifted our focus to Joe's abilities. What did he do well at home? What made him happy? What did he enjoy doing? He was fantastic at loading and unloading a dishwasher, setting the table, emptying garbage cans, and dusting his bedroom. Could any of those skills translate into a job within the community?

All our discussions came to one fact: he loved to go grocery shopping with us, and to push the shopping carts. We began talking enthusiastically with Joe about working at the grocery store, as if to plant the seed in his brain. Some of our subliminal messages such as, "Wouldn't it be fun to work there?" "You would be so good at working there." "They would love to have you working at their grocery store," began to sink in, and Joe was showing a genuine interest.

I waited for a Saturday morning when I knew Joe would be refreshed and in a good mood. On the way to the grocery store that he was very familiar with, I talked about good manners, smiling, and only handshakes. I introduced Joe to the store manager, telling him that Joe would love to work at his store. I asked if they would entertain the idea of Joe working there, and that he was real awesome at pushing grocery carts. Immediately the store manager said, "Absolutely! We could use another cart runner. Would you like to do that Joe?"

Joe replied yes and shook his hand. That would be the last handshake he would get from Joe. Since then, it has been only hugs.

Next, I contacted his supervisor at the production plant, and we worked out an agreement that they would provide one-on-one job coaching for Joe at the grocery store. The job coach would drive him to the store, provide guidance and assistance with all the rules and expectations of the grocery store, as well as his job responsibilities, and also drive him home after his shift. Joe would work for one hour a day on Monday, Tuesday, and Thursday afternoon.

A couple of weeks later, I took Joe to the store training for all new hires. A dozen other new employees were hired for positions in various departments. When the store manager asked everyone to introduce themselves, Joe said his name and eyed up the cute gal to his left. Joe yawned while representatives from human resources talked about insurance, vacation, and the like. Just as they were beginning to wrap up the meeting and ask for questions, it happened. Joe let out a big gasser. I was mortified. The others did all they could to stifle their laughter. The store manager couldn't stop laughing. Joe flatly said, "Sorry about that; that is my bottom."

Joe's first day on the job at the grocery store was May 19, 2008. He continues to work at both jobs. Reducing the number of hours he works at the production plant has proven to be beneficial in regard to his behavior. He works there in the morning and leaves for the grocery store job shortly after the lunch hour.

His responsibilities include removing garbage that may have been left in the cart, pushing the carts in the cart corrals together to make it easier for his coworker to operate the remote electric cart mover, and taking other carts into the cart garage. His job coach reminds him to watch for traffic and to be careful to not bump into any parked cars with the carts. The job coach's most difficult task is to get Joe to move no more than seven carts at a time. Always one to challenge the rules, he would rather take more.

Most of Joe's cart-running coworkers are high school boys. These young men are so kind, so patient, and so good to Joe. They understand they will be doing most of the work. They hold no resentment toward him when he doesn't pick up the slack or work faster. Along with Joe's job coach, they make sure he drinks enough water or that he takes a break from the summer heat or that he has some hot chocolate or warms up in the bitter winter cold. They do their best to carry on conversations or give Joe a high five. If they see Joe in a setting outside of work, they come to greet him. These remarkable young men are truly accepting of Joe. It is a great life lesson for them to have the opportunity to work with someone like Joe, or any other person with a disability. And Joe benefits greatly from their kindness.

It makes Joe's day when he sees someone he knows while gathering carts in the parking lot. It also makes their day because it means they may get a hug from Joe.

Neil, a neighbor, and his female coworker had gone to the store to buy groceries for work and ran into Joe in the parking lot. Joe thought it was totally cool to see Neil and gave him a huge hug; then he told his job coach, "This is my best neighbor ever!" Joe helped unload the bags into the vehicle and was very polite to the coworker. Then it was another big hug for neighbor Neil before they left. For his coworker, Neil said it was like meeting a celebrity, someone she had heard so many stories about over the years.

It was raining while Joe worked pushing grocery carts. When I came home from work I asked him if he got soaking wet while working. He said, "No, it's fine. I waterproof!"

Yet, on another day, it was raining very hard while Joe was collecting grocery carts. Fed up with his eye glasses and face getting all wet, he announced, "I fire myself!" and refused to continue working for the day.

Joe found a purse left in one of the grocery carts. His job coach instructed him to take it into the store to the service desk. As he went back out to the parking lot to continue working, a frantic woman asked Joe if he found a purse. He said, "Yes, I do. I take it in there." The woman retrieved her purse at the store's service counter, found Joe gathering more carts and gave him a $5 bill. When the job coach took Joe home, they told Paul the story and called me at work right away to tell me the good news. Then Joe called our daughter, Beth. When Beth asked what he was going to do with the five dollars he said, "Buy pizza!" One thankful woman, one proud job coach and store manager, one elated brother just waiting to buy a pizza one day soon…priceless!

Adult Years: Age Twenty-two–Forty-eight

Joe was doing his job in the parking lot and noticed a mother struggling with her young screaming son. Joe immediately went up to the boy and said, "Your behavior is not very nice, and you should be nice to your mother."

The boy screamed at Joe, saying, "Shut up!"

Joe immediately, in a calm manner, pointed at the little boy and said, "You don't talk to your mother like that, or me. You don't get Mario tonight!" The boy stopped right in his tracks and didn't say a word. Flustered by the little boy's wayward behavior, Joe began to take the cart with the groceries still in it. The mother said to Joe, "No, I need to put them in the car!"

Joe said, "You need help, I've got this for you!" and he put her groceries in her car.

You see, during his free time when Joe works at the production plant, he can play a Mario Brothers video arcade game, thus the source of the Mario reference to the little boy. I'm guessing the staff uses the Mario game as leverage for Joe's own bad behavior.

In a birthday card from his grocery store supervisor was a scratch-off card with which Joe won a 20-ounce bottle of soda. A few weeks later Joe came home from work with a package of soda cans. Forgetting about the scratch-off coupon for a bottle of soda, we struggled to figure out how the purchase came to be. We knew he did not have money with him. He told us that Ellie, his job coach, gave him a gift card for soda. When Ellie told Joe he could pick out a bottle of soda, Joe insisted that he did not drink bottled soda—only cans, which are not sold individually. The store supervisor felt bad for Joe, so they gave him a 12-pack of cans to bring home. In his thank you note to the store, Joe also included the payment for the 12-pack of soda. What a manipulator.

We are so grateful to this grocery company for allowing Joe to work at their store as a cart runner. Their expectations of Joe are no less than that of their other employees. Well, that is not entirely true. I'm guessing most of their other employees do not give their supervisor a hug when having their yearly performance review, or when they leave their shift for the day.

Joe takes so much pride in his job. It doesn't matter if he is setting his work clothes out the night before, clocking in for his shift, or gathering carts, he is so proud and looks so forward to going to work there. Simply put, Joe is living the dream.

Chapter 5

STORIES OF JOE: OUT AND ABOUT

These are a collection of separate incidents involving Joe that happened over a period of time.

As a young boy, Joe loved to make Oscar the Grouch sundaes: vanilla ice cream, chocolate syrup, peanut butter, and pickles.

At his favorite restaurant, Joe ordered a separate plate of pickles. The server obliged. Halfway through the plate of pickles, Joe realized they were not the dill pickles he was used to; they were garlic pickles. He didn't eat pickles for a long time after that.

Joe loved the Bluffside, a neighborhood bar. He would sneak out of the house as often as he could to walk or ride his bicycle the four or five blocks over four lanes of traffic and a busy railroad track to get there. Fortunately, the owner and bartenders knew Joe and his family, as did many of the patrons. So, Joe felt very comfortable there.

Joe would often say to our dad, "Hey Jim, you-me together—go to the Bluff and drink!"

Several family members were in town for a wedding and went to the Bluffside with Joe, age nineteen, in tow. When a sister's back was turned Joe guzzled her full glass of beer, got goofy, and started doing impressions such as Billy Crystal's "Dah-ling, you look mah-velous" and James Cagney's "You dirty rat, you." He was quite the entertainer that night.

The neighborhood tavern wasn't the only place where Joe felt he had the right to be on the other side of the bar helping customers. Once I took him to an ice cream parlor to get an ice cream cone. I turned my head for mere seconds; then heard the employee shout, "No, no, no," as she pried his hands off the soft-serve ice cream machine. Vanilla and chocolate swirl was coming out of the machine with full force. Joe had skirted under the counter to help the workers get his cone. It was an extra-large cone for him that day. Coincidentally, he still asks for a large cone.

When ordering a sandwich Joe would say, "I'll have a BLT—no bacon, no lettuce."

For a long time, we struggled to get Joe to eat vegetables. Thinking I was being quite clever, I chopped carrots into tiny pieces using a food chopper and added them to the ingredients for the enchiladas. At dinner, Joe's plate was full of tiny little carrots that he had spit out, which I had told him was cheddar cheese. There was no fooling him. Lesson learned. From then on, I have made certain to steam the carrots and all other vegetables that I sneak into his foods.

When planning the menu for the following week, Joe said, "How about long-hair noodles?" It took me a few minutes to figure out what he meant was Angel Hair pasta.

As we walked into the restaurant bar, several people were sitting at the bar, mostly men. Joe took two steps in and approached a big burly guy with a mustache and full beard. Joe gently grabbed him on the chin and said, "Hey there Scruffy, how are you doing?" None of the guys even questioned it. They just laughed and said hello to Joe as he found a seat at the other side of the bar.

Without our knowledge, Joe had been taking money from home and buying candy bars at work. One day he came home from work with a pocket full of candy wrappers. After counting out nine wrappers that he had eaten that day, we made certain he didn't take any more money to work. Soon his job coach noticed that he stopped bringing money and was unable to buy candy bars. One day as she walked past the vending area she saw Joe, his cheek pressed firmly against the glass front of the vending machine, as his hand made circles on the glass. When she approached and asked what he was doing, he sadly told her that he "just misses them."

As we entered a Colorado town and passed a McDonald's, my hungry brother said, "WOW, a McDonald's. What a town!" Then we passed a Denny's, "Wow, a Denny's. This place is special!"

Joe tossed his container of strawberries all over the lunchroom at his work. When staff asked him why, he said the lunchroom staff sat him in the wrong spot at the table, and, "I don't like strawberries. They make me jumpy inside my tummy." He also said strawberries, "make me feel nervous." I would be nervous too if I were him and had to come home and face my disappointment over his wasted food. He wanted applesauce, not strawberries.

I received a voicemail message from Scott, the behavioral specialist at Joe's work. He stated that a staff member, knowing Joe should not be purchasing from the vending machine, alerted him that Joe was eating a Danish in the vending area. When Scott followed up with him, Joe didn't want to tell him where he got money to buy the Danish and wouldn't say much else other than "mind your own f***ing business." Scott asked if I was aware he had money with him.

When I got home from work I asked Joe about the "Danish" he ate. He was indignant as he corrected me, "It NOT a Danish. It a sweet roll."

What do you get when you take $45 that was set aside for Girl Scout cookies? If you are Joe, you get one Snickers, two big cookies, three HoHos, and you're finally busted as another $5 bill was going into the vending machine.

I get a clean bathroom and other chores done, and a brother who can't stop sucking up to me. He also said, "Well, I 45 years young—I take $45 dollars, you know."

Joe had just finished his bottle of orange Sunkist. He let out a big sigh and said, "Spicy! It tastes minty!"

We were in a very small South Dakota town. Food options were extremely limited. I suggested we just go to the pizza place.

Joe: "No! Pizza is bad for your waist. Let's eat a burger instead."

At work I received an email from one of Joe's supervisors. He was found eating Cheetos, still in the original packaging, but half eaten by someone else. Joe had taken them out of the garbage in the lunch room. My question: Who *doesn't* eat all their Cheetos?

Every now and again, there is a Peanut Butter Bandit at our house. We know this because first, he will leave fork marks all around on the peanut butter. Then, with his finger as far down into the jar as he can reach, he will swipe around the edges. Finally, there will be smudges of peanut butter all around the outside of the jar and on the lid as he closes it. Ironically, the PB Bandit only strikes when Joe is off on Friday, and while I am at work.

Joe was home alone for an hour. When I got home, there was peanut butter on both sides of Joe's mouth.

"Did you have peanut butter for supper?"

Joe: "No" (wiping off the side of his mouth).

"Did you have any peanut butter tonight?"

Joe: "Nope. No peanut butter" (looking at his hand with the peanut butter on it). "None at all. Nope."

"Did you use a spoon or a fork to eat the peanut butter?"

Joe: "My pointy finger."

Shining a flashlight in each of the rooms, Joe told me. "I protect the house. I do detective work when you are not here. It is all clear. See, the peanut butter is safe. I protect it."

Whew. Good to know. I'll be able to sleep tonight knowing the peanut butter is safe!

To save time, Paul and I make Joe's lunch for work the night before. As I was making it one evening he said, "I have a Miller Lite, no Diet Sierra Mist."

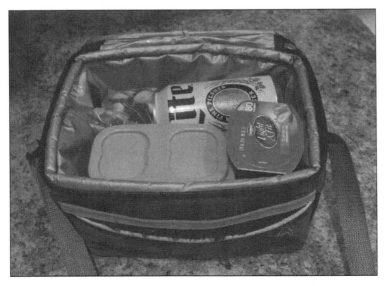

Joe's lunch box after he "substituted" his beverage of choice.

I explained to him he could not have beer in his lunch for work. He insisted it was okay and said, "It fine. I like it. I drink it."

Thinking the conversation was over I zipped up his lunch box and put it in the refrigerator for the night. The next morning, I recalled our conversation, opened the lunchbox, and sure enough, there sat a Miller Lite. He got up during the night and exchanged the soda for the beer.

On Thursdays, if Joe follows his behavioral plan at work, he can have two dollars for the vending machine as his reward (it also keeps him from plugging the vending machine with bills from my purse). One day I noticed a few coins on the bookcase shelving above the desk in his bedroom. He came in as I was counting it. He said, "Don't touch it, I give it to Claire for a tip." She works at the restaurant/bar where we frequently go for dinner. Joe loves Claire so much, and it is good incentive throughout the week for him to follow the behavioral plan.

The restaurant/bar doesn't have chocolate milk, so Joe brings his own. Before we leave the house, Joe is careful to remember his small bottle of chocolate milk and the coins he has saved for a tip. Once we get to the bar, Joe turns over his milk to the bartender where they keep it in the cooler until his dinner is served. When his dinner bill is paid he takes out the handful of coins for Claire and tells her, "Here's your tip, Claire. Keep the change, you filthy animal."

Joe, to the young gals who made his lunch at the diner: "The sandwich was really good. How about you come to my house. We go on a date. Bring your checkbook." The girls were still laughing as we left.

Joe tends to leave a lasting impression with others at restaurants, especially in the bar area. He often will grab some random guy, someone he has never met, as he enters the bar, and give him the biggest bear hug ever. Or, he'll go down the line of seated patrons and give all the men a handshake or a big hug and give the women a kiss on the back of her hand or on her cheek. The reaction of others is very heartwarming, and they welcome it. You can see on some faces that they cannot wait for it to be their turn. It's very sweet.

Paul and I went to a favorite restaurant/bar without Joe. At this place we generally eat our dinner at the bar. Shortly before we left, Ken came up to us and asked where Joe was. We were stunned because we had been joking earlier that no one would recognize us because Joe wasn't with us. Ken went on to share a story of the last time we were there, and he sat next to Joe. Joe was eyeing up Ken's macaroni and cheese and tater tots. Joe was telling him how good his mac and cheese and tater tots looked. Joe said to Ken, "I have fish, and tartar sauce, and French fries, and coleslaw," like he was downtrodden and sad about it. Ken described exactly how Joe placed his order for dinner to the server. Then he shared how I was nit-picking Joe to "leave him alone, move over here, just let him eat, etc." I remembered the scene exactly as he described it. It was a good lesson for me. What I thought of as Joe pestering the man while he ate his dinner was not at all how the man perceived it. They were connecting as new buddies over macaroni and cheese and tater tots.

Animals, Aquariums, and Zoos

Bitten by a llama, splashed by a stingray, swam with the dolphins, hissed at the badgers, attempted to climb the bear cage, and kissed many, many dogs.

Joe took endless trips to Myrick Park Zoo, a city park less than a mile from our parents' home. The park had swings, slides, monkey bars, merry-go-rounds, and other assorted park equipment, along with picnic tables and grassy areas for family gatherings. In the lower section of the park was a very small zoo of sorts, with a small menagerie of animals: two bears, deer, badgers, foxes, raccoons, groundhogs, small monkeys, ducks, rabbits, peacocks, and a few other caged birds. This was one of Joe's favorite places where he would come when he would sneak out of the house and hop on his bicycle. He enjoyed all the animals, but the badgers were his favorite.

He would stand at the badger cage for what seemed like hours and hiss at them until the badgers reciprocated with a hiss back to Joe. He was beyond delighted when the badgers hissed back at him, and so was the person who was responsible for Joe at the time—so we could finally move on to the next animal.

Of course, all the animals were fenced in. Fortunately, the bear cage had metal fencing over the top of it and the cage was very high, because during one of Joe's climbing-on-everything phases, he attempted to climb on the top of the bear cage. He succeeded several times in climbing into the duck pond area, but there were no worries about the ducks. The park employees were on a first-name basis with us because they had to unlock and open the gate each time to let Joe out of the duck cage. Also, it is not that we were not attentive to Joe while at the zoo, he was just so fast and could slither out of the grasp we had on his wrist.

Shortly after Buster, the family dog, died, someone came over to the house and, not knowing, asked Joe where Buster was. Joe said, "Hit the road. On the highway to heaven."

Joe and his dog, Buster.

At least twelve of us were lined up along a fence to see the llamas at a friend's farm. The owner explained about her llamas, their temperament, what they ate, that they sometimes spit at people, but that they were very friendly. Joe's excitement was building as the first llama walked along the fence past each of us, stopping to sniff our hands, or just to check us out and let us pet them. As soon as it got to Joe, the llama leaned in close and bit Joe on his upper chest. Immediately, Joe yelled, "Stupid F***ing llama!" We could not stop laughing, and Joe could not stop swearing or scolding the llama. We felt a little bad once we realized Joe had red swelling and clearly defined llama teeth marks on his chest. We were prepared to be spit at by the llamas, but not to be bitten by one. As luck would have it, it could only have happened to Joe.

One weekend while Joe visited our daughter, Beth, in Minneapolis, they visited Underwater World at the Mall of America in Bloomington, Minnesota. After walking through and seeing all the fish and shark exhibits, there is an area where you can touch small sharks and stingrays. Beth went over to an area where visitors could wash their hands before and after touching the stingrays while Joe stayed over by the pool of stingrays. When she returned, Joe was soaking wet from his head to his waist. Joe said one of the stingrays splashed him. Needless to say, Joe cussed out the stingrays the rest of the weekend and hasn't touched them since.

Church Stories

We lived two blocks away from the church. It was a familiar place to Joe as he went there for Mass with family, to weddings, funerals, and at other times, just to visit.

The parish priest relayed this story:

Joe's dad was looking for Joe who was somewhere in the area of the church. Mass was being held at the time. Suddenly everyone was startled when Joe came into the side door of the church on his bicycle, rode down the side aisle, and out the front door.

He was also known to have walked the family dog, a Boston terrier named Buster, through the church a time or two as a baptism or funeral was taking place.

When putting money in the collection basket Joe would say, "Keep the change!"

On a cold November Sunday, Mom and Dad were at 7:30 a.m. Mass. On his way back from Communion, Dad spotted nineteen-year-old Joe on the other side of church, also coming back from Communion. When Dad went over to catch him, he noticed the colorful pair of plaid pants he was wearing. He didn't recognize the pants, but upon closer inspection realized that Joe was wearing his pajamas, shoes with no socks, and his jacket.

Joe was twenty-four-years old. Mom and Dad were leaving church after early-morning Mass. Dad said, "There's Joe!" Mom looked for his green jacket and blue jeans because it was still cool in the mornings, but instead she saw Joe standing on the street corner, wearing only his eyeglasses and a bright pink towel held together tightly at his backside. He had just taken a shower and was left to get dressed while Mom and Dad went to Mass. Instead, naked and wrapped only in the towel, Joe had walked the two blocks to church to find Mom and Dad. It was quite a sight from the rear, no doubt.

Always intrigued by the flames of the devotion candles, he would take every opportunity he could to blow them out. One time it backfired on him though because he blew so hard the candle wax splattered all over his face and eyebrows. Thank goodness, his eyeglasses protected his eyes.

The scariest story of Joe in church was when he snuck out of the house and walked over to the church. Fortunately, a custodian spotted him just as he took several church bulletins and lit them on fire with the flame from the devotion candles.

Swimmer Joe

Joe learned to swim at a very early age. Like his older siblings, he took swim lessons at the country club. The shallow end of the kids' swimming pool was about two feet deep, while the deep end was about ten feet. When he was tall enough and legs sturdy enough, he would stand in the shallow section. Eventually he would put his face in the water and blow bubbles, hold on to the edge and kick his legs, or annoy other kids by splashing water at them, especially when he discovered they didn't like to be splashed. Often, he would occupy one of the two corners to play with his toys or a Nerf ball. He especially enjoyed watching the water go down the drains around the edges of the pool.

He took to the water like a frog to a pond. In fact, he resembled a frog when swimming: eyes wide open, legs kicking like the back legs of a frog. He grew to be an excellent swimmer. When he tired of swimming, he'd simply sit on one of the ladders and not let others use it until Mom or one of his older sisters would wrap him up in a towel and say it was time to rest.

Once a child could swim the width of the pool, the lifeguard would grant them permission to jump off the small board in the ten-foot section. Joe passed the test and began going off the board, swimming to the ladder on either side of the deep end. He discovered a whole new world once he was able to jump off the board—the filter system at the bottom of the pool. He would jump off the board over and over, butting in line to be next off the board. His goal was to get to the filter system. The older he got, the deeper he could jump, and the longer he could hold his breath underwater.

Finally, the day came. Joe jumped off the board, swam to the bottom, holding his breath underwater longer than most kids, and he lifted the grate cover off the filter system. It took grit and determination, but he did it. He removed the cover. Lifeguards blew their whistles, and everyone was ordered out of the pool. It would take two lifeguards to properly replace the filter cover. From that day forward, the lifeguards never quite trusted Joe. He tested out of the kids' pool and was now able to swim in the big pool with the adults and his older siblings. He loved going down the slide, tossing the water-filled Nerf ball, especially when it hit someone in the head, and playing chase. Usually it was Joe being chased and laughing like crazy until he was caught on the other side of the pool.

Twelve-year-old Joe slept overnight at Paul's and my home. About mid-morning he snuck out of the house. Paul and I searched the neighborhood for him. Soon we spotted him walking toward home through the backyards of three of our neighbors. We instinctively knew where he had been. He was dripping wet up to his chest. Our neighbors down the street had an above-ground pool, which was always covered with a tarp when not in use. He climbed up the three steps to the deck, opened one side of the cover and went for a swim. We talked to our neighbors right away to let them know what had happened and to apologize, letting them know it would not happened again. The neighbors were frantic because they thought their pool was child-proof. Little did they know it wasn't Joe-proof.

As a young teen, and for only a short time, Joe was involved with the local Special Olympics. With his swimming skills, it was the obvious sport of choice. He practiced with the team and participated in several swim meets. At one particular meet his swim coach thought he could win a blue ribbon easily as his swimming skills rivaled those of a dolphin. However, Joe is not the competitive type, and to him, winning is much less meaningful than showing off for a crowd. Rather than swimming directly down the lane doing the front crawl, Joe entertained the crowd by turning somersaults, rolling over onto his back, spitting fountains of water and waving to the crowd. All that and he still beat the competition.

At a restaurant, Paul and I struck up a conversation with the bartender. Brad was a physical education major at one of the universities in town. When I asked Brad if he had ever taught the special education kids at the Saturday morning program he said, "Yes, I almost got drowned by one." Paul asked if he knew nineteen-year-old Joe Burns. Brad said, "Yes! That is the one who almost drowned me! He jumped on my back as I was swimming—he is strong!" When Brad and Joe got out of the pool, Brad proceeded to threaten to call Joe's mom about what happened. Brad said, "Joe turns into a good little boy when Mom's around. Yeah, just tell him you're going to tell his mom what he did or said, and he will behave right away!"

Joe would often spend the weekend with our daughter, Beth, and a favorite thing of Joe's was to go to the waterpark. He especially enjoyed the tube slide. After several trips up the stairs and down the slide, the little girl who had been ahead of them each time couldn't take her eyes off Joe. Finally, she asked Beth who was in her twenties, "Is he your husband?" Beth told her no, that he is her uncle. "Oh," she said, and down the slide she went. She probably wondered why her uncle wasn't cool like Joe and go to the waterpark with her.

Doctor Joe

Joe worked at one of the local hospitals for a brief time when he was in his young twenties. Someone asked him how he liked working at the hospital. "Just call me doctor," he said coolly.

Others go to work and never expect a hug or kiss, but wherever Joe goes, a hug is sure to follow.

At his eye appointment, Joe lavished the medical assistant with sweet nothings. After the physician completed Joe's eye exam and was preparing to leave the room, he offered his well wishes and extended his hand to shake. Joe shook the doctor's hand, then pulled him in, giving him a big bear hug. The look on the doctor's face was priceless. Joe had him in such a tight embrace, with the doctor's arms straight down along his sides, he could hardly move. Judging from his reaction, I am going to guess that was the first bear hug the physician had received from a patient in a long time. The gals at the hair salon are used to Joe's hugs goodbye—the eye doctor? Not so much!

Joe was about forty when I took him for his yearly physical. The doctor performed a prostate exam, Joe's first. As we walked down the hallway to have lab work done, Joe questioned, "Why he stick his finger in my butt?" I had to distract his attention and change the subject quickly as we were only ten feet from the lab's crowded waiting room, and I didn't want to have to answer that question one more time in front of a room full of strangers.

I was called by Joe's work at the production plant that Joe had been spitting and swearing at another coworker, and he need to be tested for hepatitis within a certain time frame. Livid with him for spitting and swearing, I ask the phlebotomist to, "take out all the swear words, all the spitting, and all the poor behavior" from Joe's arm. The woman looked up at me quizzically, and I nodded like, "Work with me here, lady, work with me." She picked up my vibes and began to admonish Joe, telling him she took out as many swear words and spitting as she could. Now each time he needs to have a blood draw he tells the phlebotomists he has "been pretty good, with no swear words."

Joe had surgery for cataracts. First, he had the right eye done and a month later he had surgery on the left eye. I learned after the first surgery to bring a pad of paper and a pen with me to the appointment, so I could record the things he said to the medical staff and the way in which he answered their questions. I was so glad I did.

Try as I might, I could barely keep it together when the nurse prepping him for surgery asked the questions she asks of most of her patients. It went exactly like this:

"Hello, my name is Britney."

"Are you Britney Spears? You are wonderful. You are one terrific girl!"

"Can you spell your name?"

"S-a-n-d-r-a and J-o-e."

"Do you have dentures?"

Stretching his lips and mouth out as far as he could, while also sticking out his tongue, he said, "No! I not wear dentures. Why you ask if I wear dentures? I not old. Do I look like I wear dentures?"

"How tall are you Joe?"

"Forty-five pounds."

"Are you diabetic?"

"I am not going to die!"

"How are your bowels? Do you have any issues going to the bathroom?"

"My penis and testicles are in my pants."

A short time later another staffer came in the room and told Joe he was going to be moved to what they refer to as a "holding room." With all the police and jail-type of shows he watches on television, he mistook her for saying a "holding cell." In a very defensive manner, he said, "Holding cell? I say nice, kind words. I say kind words to my sister. If I don't say nice, kind words, don't say anything at all." I think he was trying to convince me and the hospital staffer that he would talk nice to me—and that he was fearful he was going to be taken to jail and locked up.

I consider the left eye cataract surgery more successful than his right eye. At least he didn't angrily ask me, "Why you let the nurse poke me in the eye with a needle?"

Joe is surprisingly very healthy. So many with Down syndrome have heart or other medical issues. With that said, he twice had very serious health issues. At four months of age he was in the hospital for five days, in an oxygen tent, for pneumonia. The second time was at age twenty-nine. He had just begun living with me and my family full time when I took Joe to the doctor for an illness. I was given a prescription for liquid penicillin for him. I was about to give Joe his third dose of the medication and quickly noticed his body was covered in red spots. At that point I ever so vaguely remembered many years earlier my mom stating he was severely allergic to penicillin. I rushed him to the clinic just in the nick of time. His throat was nearly closed. Boy, did that doctor scold me. I felt horrible for not remembering something so serious about him.

Traveling Joe

One thing I never feel horrible about is taking Joe with us as we travel. Overall, he is a very easy traveler. He will gladly go for a car ride or hop on an airplane for a cross-country vacation. Growing up, our family vacations consisted of a car ride to visit relatives in Wisconsin and Minneapolis, or a short trip to the Milwaukee Zoo. Once the older kids were on their own or married, my parents would take Joe to visit them or visit friends in Florida.

After Joe came to live with my family, we included him in many of our travels. In many respects he was much easier to travel with than our own kids. As long as he had food to eat, an occasional bathroom break, and music as loud as we would allow, he was fine. He never complained about the distance, someone staring at him, or being bored.

Our first travels with Joe included car rides to Colorado and Florida, and airplane rides to California to visit family. Always the charmer, he was a hit with the flight attendants, and they would lavish him with extra bags of peanuts or pretzels.

In 2008, when Joe was thirty-seven years old, Paul and I took him to Arizona. In Sedona we went on one of the famed Pink Jeep Tours. It was a high adventure, off-road tour of the spectacular red-rock outback country to the Diamondback Gulch and ancient ruins in a hot pink jeep that held about eight people, but on this tour, it was just the driver, Joe, Paul, and me. Joe insisted he would sit in the front seat. He loved every bump and bounce of the rough-and-rocky off-road trails.

Then it happened. Three twenty-something guys in a little yellow Tom Car crashed into us as they nearly flew over the blind crest at the top of the trail that intersected the trail we were on. Once our driver verified everyone was fine, and that the only damage was a flat tire on our Jeep, Joe yelled out to the three men, "Are you insane? You are a crazy driver! You crashed into us. What are you thinking?" He continued to scold them until we parted ways. Joe would not stop talking about the accident and demanded to know their names. Not knowing, we simply threw out three random names. For days he would continue to talk about the three in their yellow Tom Car crashing into us. Secretly, we knew he loved every minute of the accident, and the Pink Jeep tour was the highlight of the trip for him.

It was on this trip that I learned what a good photographer Joe was. I had my first digital camera and asked Joe to take a photo of Paul and me. With his poor eyesight, instead of looking into the viewfinder, the digital camera allowed him to not only see us but also center us on the display screen before pressing the shutter. He has since taken many photos, some of them very impressive.

Moving on, we went to Williams, Arizona, the gateway to the Grand Canyon National Park. We boarded a train for the two-and-a-half-hour ride to the Grand Canyon. We had often talked about taking Joe on a train, and this proved to be an enjoyable ride, that is, until the train ride back to Williams. Cowboys on horseback rode alongside the slow-moving train with bandanas covering their nose and mouth, firing off blanks from their six-shooters, staging a "train robbery." They hopped on the train, "robbing" passengers of their money and valuables. One of their cohorts, a woman, ran down the aisle screaming that there were robbers on the train. She ran past Joe screaming. He was sitting in an aisle seat. The woman was followed closely by one of the "robbers," and as he ran toward her, Joe stuck his arm straight out across the aisle and shouted "NO!" The "robber" was stopped cold in his tracks, doubling over at the waist with a groan. He was stunned. He said that had never happened to him before. It took days to convince Joe it was all just a make-believe game.

He is very protective of women, whether they are being picked on, called names, or being chased by fake train robbers.

Not being one to venture too far away from us, whether in a grocery store or in a public place such as the Grand Canyon, we were humored by Joe's newfound independence. Paul and I were absorbing the powerful and inspiring beauty of the magnificent South Rim of the Grand Canyon. Joe seemed to really enjoy the landscape as well. We were in no hurry and took our time taking photographs. Soon Joe began to inch his way farther and farther from us, walking past other groups, yet still in our sight. To the amusement of both of us and other visitors, each time he walked a few feet away he would say, "Hey Sis, I am over here. Can you see me?" I would wave and respond positively. He would continue on, taking a few steps and calling out to me for reassurance that indeed I could still see him, until he was about twenty to thirty yards away. That must have been his limit because he then sat down and waited for us to catch up to him. As we approached he proudly said, "Do you see me? I walk far away!"

The first time we took Joe with us to Cabo San Lucas, Mexico, we also went with another sister and her family. It was a grand time with the days spent on the beach, wading in the Sea of Cortez, swimming in the pool, being "buried" in the sand, and relaxing on the beach chairs, Joe with his iPod on singing his favorite Styx song, *Mr. Roboto*, at the top of his lungs without a care in the world. This was the life, and he was loving it, far away from freezing cold and snowy Wisconsin.

By the end of the week Joe had no problems telling the locals selling their wares, "No, gracias." Often, he would tell them to get lost or take a hike, but with a smile on his face. He had no trouble summoning a server for another strawberry smoothie. He walked with our sister to the room for a short break, to gather snacks, and to make a "good" margarita. She handed Joe her strawberry margarita to hold while she momentarily went to another room. In the less than sixty seconds that she was gone, Joe drank the entire margarita. Wiping his mouth, he said, "Mmm, mmm!" He took an extended nap on the beach that afternoon.

Joe is not wired to be fearful, nervous, or with a sense of impending danger so he was happy to follow the crowd when they went parasailing,

Troublemaker the dolphin giving Joe a kiss.

riding on an eight-person banana boat raft, or swimming with the dolphins. In fact, swimming with the dolphins was one of the highlights of his trip. The dolphin assigned to his group was aptly named "Troublemaker." Joe listened attentively to the trainer's instructions. He performed all the signs the trainer gave to have Troublemaker dance, take him for a ride while holding its dorsal fins, and to get a kiss, and another kiss, and another kiss. It was another moment in his life where it seemed as though the dolphin and Joe were keenly aware of each other; as if they had a special bond understood by only the two of them.

It didn't matter if we were on the beach, walking through the resort lobby, at a restaurant, or shopping for souvenirs, everyone treated Joe as though he was a rock star and we were his entourage. Employees, guests, and locals would wave, smile, hug, or offer a high-five greeting to Joe wherever we went. He was a rock star, indeed.

Taking a break from the beach, we spent an afternoon down by the marina and shopping for Mexican handicrafts. Never one to be in a hurry, Joe lagged behind as we walked from shop to shop. At one point, Joe was about ten feet behind us. We heard a hearty greeting of "Hola, Amigo!" As we turned around to look, Joe was giving one of the local men a great big bear hug, saying "Hola, how are you?" The man had a smile from ear to ear, as if they were long-lost friends.

As we went through the Mexican airport security for our flight home, Joe was the only one of the nine of us to be pulled aside for an extra security check. The Transportation Security Agent patted Joe up and down, checking for contraband, weapons, or the like. As the agent patted Joe's tummy and waist, Joe broke out in a hilarious giggle, saying, "You TICKLE me!" The rest of us waiting for him got a dirty look from the agent for erupting in laughter. We knew the second Joe was pulled aside what was going to happen, and it did, much to our amusement.

Respite Weekends with the BODS

Respite care is a temporary short-term period of time to provide caregivers a break from the daily routine, challenges, and stress of caring for individuals with a disability or for those caring for an aging adult. In our case, it is a time for Paul and me to have a break from Joe and vice versa. When we need a break, Joe stays at the home of one of two sisters and their husbands, or at our daughter Beth and her husband Brian's home. Generally, it only takes the weekend for us to feel refreshed and renewed to continue to provide Joe with the compassionate and constant care he deserves.

However, since June 2001, for one weekend every month, we have also provided respite care for Steve. In 2013, we invited Randy to join us for respite weekends. Steve dubbed Joe, Randy, and another friend, Mark, all friends since early childhood, all about the same age, and all with Down syndrome, the BODS, Brothers of Down syndrome. Our intentions for providing respite care for Steve and Randy was to offer Joe the opportunity to continue their friendship, and for Joe to continue to develop his socialization skills with someone other than his own family. We all need a good friend, and the BODS are no different. Some weekends Mark comes over for the day to hang out with the other three and to participate in the activities we plan, but he does not stay overnight like the other two.

Since they were three years old, Joe and Steve have been friends and were classmates through all their school years. While similar in height, weight, hair color, and all the unique features that are characteristic of a person with Downs, they are as different as they are alike. As schoolchildren, people would often confuse the one for the other. Both took the name mix-up in stride and would correct the person when mistaken. However, if it was something mischievous that Joe was doing or had done, Steve was very quick to point out, "I am not Joe Burns. He has glasses, I don't!"

It is interesting to see their differences: Joe loves writing numbers, Steve loves watching wrestling videos; Joe is slow as molasses in nearly everything he does, Steve is quick, punctual, and always ready when called; Joe is wayward or defiant, Steve is always on his best behavior. But seat them next to each other, and they turn into goofy little pre-teen boys. They call each other names such as cow or pig. They poke each other in the belly or hit one another with a pillow. All the while they are laughing and enjoying each other's company.

Mealtime conversations with Joe and Steve are always good for a laugh. One evening Steve bragged that he was the smartest person in his high school class. Paul said, "Okay, Mr. Smarty Pants, what is six plus six?"
Quickly Steve replied, "Sixty-six."
Joe retorted, "Steve, that is not right."
Paul then asked Joe what six plus six equals.
Confidently, Joe responded, "Seven!"

When they are sent outside to take a walk through our subdivision, it takes them twice as long as it should because they stop about every ten steps to gently kick each other in the butt, knock each other's baseball cap off their head, call each other silly names, and then embrace in a big bear hug. This continues for most of the walk, much to the amusement of the neighbors because it is quite comical.

Steve and Joe embracing on their walk.

But then comes the night when Joe will wake Steve up at three o'clock in the morning by turning on his bedroom light. Steve will tell Joe to turn off the light and go back to bed, and Joe will. In the morning before Steve has a chance to tattle on Joe, and he often does, Joe will either deny any wrongdoing during the night, or he will tell me about it and think it was the funniest thing ever. Either way, we always find out, and it generally results in Joe being reprimanded by having to shake rugs, scrub a toilet, or vacuum his bedroom.

The summer we moved into our new neighborhood, Joe and Steve were sent out for a walk. They had been gone for at least an hour when Paul heard talking in the front of the house. He went to the door and saw a police officer standing on the front porch with Joe and Steve. The police department had received a phone call from someone in the subdivision who had never seen these two before and was concerned they might be lost. The police officer asked them where they lived. Joe said his standard reply of, "I don't know," while Steve simply clammed up and didn't respond at all. The officer then checked their identification cards and neither showed the city where we now live. Also, neither knew the name of the street in which we now lived. The officer had Joe and Steve get into her police car and drove around the subdivision going up and down the streets, turning whichever way Joe pointed until she was on the right street and at the right house. Both were so scared that they would be in trouble. Joe's eyes flitted back and forth as fast as a hummingbird's wings.

Once back home, neither appreciated our singing of the television show *COPS'* theme song, "Bad boys, bad boys, whatcha gonna do?"

We tend to plan activities for Joe, Steve, and Randy, often out in the community, for two reasons. First, it is good for them to feel and be accepted in the community by doing and experiencing what the average person can do. Second, it is vitally important for the general population to see and understand that these gentlemen are no different than them. Their abilities may vary and their approach to an activity may sometimes be unconventional, but they prove to themselves and to others that they can do it—and be so proud of themselves while doing it.

One example of this was when I took Joe, Steve, Randy, and Mark to paint a picture on canvas at a local art store in our downtown area. All four, initially not too excited and all very hesitant to paint, donned aprons, and with paintbrushes in hand, painted an ice cream cone masterpiece. Their creativity and joyfulness while painting was remarkable. When we were finished, each proudly carried their painted canvas as we walked down the block where I treated them to an ice cream cone. We sat outside on this warm July day eating our ice cream and chattering about how much fun it was to paint the pictures. Several people smiled as they passed by at the sight of four gentlemen with Down syndrome eating ice cream cones with their respective ice cream cone paintings resting next to them.

We have done many other activities in the community such as playing miniature golf, playing games at an arcade and entertainment center, visiting a longhorn cattle ranch, going to a wilderness park and zoo in a nearby city, and of course, their favorite, dining out at a restaurant. Closer to home, the BODS enjoy bean bag toss (the neighbors also enjoy watching them play), taking walks, having a picnic lunch outside on the deck, Bingo, and what we call the Indoor Winter Olympic games, various made-up games to keep them active and having fun together during Wisconsin's coldest winter months.

Steve, one of the Brothers of Down syndrome (BODS), had his bedroom door locked overnight. While I took a walk outside, Joe went downstairs to Steve's bedroom, poked a pair of little orange scissors in the lock and rattled the door handle until it opened. Then he turned on the bedroom light. Steve was very upset when he came upstairs for breakfast. I did all I could to not laugh when Joe eventually told me what he did, and how he opened the lock. Joe watches so many police, repo, and criminal-type television shows that he knew how to open a locked door. He is so much smarter than what we sometimes give him credit for, but that didn't stop him from having to be reprimanded and having to shake the rugs and vacuum the floor.

We were standing at the kitchen island, and I made Joe look me in the eyes when I asked him if he turned the light on in Steve's room. He would look away and say no. I kept softly saying, *Look at my eyes*. He would look and then divert his eyes. Finally, about the tenth time he looked and held the look for about 10 seconds when he confessed. But, it wasn't until about two hours later when Joe told me he used the orange scissors to unlock the door.

One summer day Paul took the guys to play miniature golf. When they came home they told me Paul was now an honorary member of the BODS. When I asked if I could be an honorary member they told me I couldn't because I'm not old enough to have Down syndrome.

At dinner, a server, other than ours, came over to Paul and me and said, "You know how you see someone and you think, 'I love him/her.' As soon as I saw you come in, I said, 'I LOVE them.'" She was referring to our precious BODs (Brothers of Down syndrome). We love them, too!

Chapter 6

"JOE-ISMS"—RANDOM FUNNY COMMENTS AND STORIES

On a summer morning, nineteen-year-old Joe left the house when Mom and Dad were at early morning Mass. He rode his bicycle to the country club via the railroad tracks. Fortunately, there were no trains at that time. Our parents were members of the country club, so he was very familiar with the area. By the tenth tee, Joe swung his bicycle toward the clubhouse, and like Evil Knievel, he rode into the pond which was near the ninth hole and the swimming pool area. Swimmers were lined up along the fence encouraging him to come out of the pond. He did, and the bicycle was still between his legs. Then he headed up the hill and over to a nearby park a quarter of a mile away where he was found soaking wet. When asked how he got so wet he replied, "I don't know."

At the country club he tried to convince the golf pro to let him take a golf cart home because he was so tired. With the golf pro's back turned, Joe took off on a cart saying, "Jim (his father) will bring it back." He didn't get too far before he was stopped. But, he still loves to drive a golf cart when he gets a chance.

Paul and I were on vacation. Joe stayed with another sister. One evening he said to her, "What you thinking? You think you my sister Sandra?"

She said, "Why, because I'm so beautiful?"

He replied, "No, because you shouting!"

He sneezed three times really hard. As he blew his nose and washed his hands with soap he said, "Whew, I had a pack of sneezes!"

Paul and I were talking with a friend who frequently drives a semi-truck from Wisconsin to Texas. He takes a truck full of cheese to Texas and brings back a truck full of bananas. Joe said, "Hmmm, cheese comes from cows."

I asked, "Where do bananas come from?"

He said, "From chickens, I think."

In the car on the way to Minneapolis, and as we were going through Rochester, Minnesota, I asked Joe: "Do you know where we are?"

Joe: "Yup."

Me: "Where are we?"

Joe: "Right here!"

Me: "Good Morning Brother! Rise and shine!"

Joe: "I NOT shining!"

After dinner, I asked: "What are you going to do now, Joe?"

Thinking he would say, "Brush my teeth," he instead said: "I'm going to wiggle my butt and dance like crazy!"

"We're supposed to get a lot of thunderstorms tonight, Joe, so if you hear the thunder, just keep sleeping."

"Nope. I HATE sleeping!"

Joe-ism's

At a luncheon after a funeral, two different people told Paul and me the exact same story, which I had never heard before. A young Joe would give women a "noogie" on their head while saying, "Hey, Sexy Grandma!" And yes, one of them was a grandma; her granddaughter told me the story.

During lunch at a sponsored trout pond fishing day for a local Down syndrome group, everyone introduced themselves. When I finished, I turned to Joe for him to introduce himself. In a voice I had never before heard, he loudly and proudly said, "Hi, I'm Charles Kuralt!" The group erupted with laughter. Hours later I asked why he said Charles Kuralt. He said, "I just kidding!"

And this my friends, is why I am writing a book about my favorite brother. Charles Kuralt had been deceased for 16 years at this time.

Me: "Joe, Aunt Lorna died yesterday."
Joe: "Dying is unacceptable behavior!"

When he wants me to make cookies he doesn't just ask me to make them. He hints around the subject by saying, "Boys like cookies, you know."

Joe scolded his niece and nephew's dog that was barking: "Barking is a terrible choice. I will teach you how to bark. All you have to do is, 'meow, meow, meow,' because barking is a terrible choice."

Joe: "Why don't you trip over your shoes? HAHAHA."
"Joe, that is not kind."
"Talk to the hand, I not listening."
"How would you like to scrub floors?"
Joe: "Come on, be my baby!"

Joe: "My bedroom door needs an oil change. It is too creaky."

Joe and I were both working individually at the table writing, doing paperwork, etc. Out of the blue he randomly said:
Joe: "Are you embarrassed?"
Me: "No, I'm not embarrassed."
Joe: "You're NOT?"

At bedtime Joe and I discuss the next night's supper and what time I will be home from work. Due to a late work function, I did not get home until 8 p.m. He told me, "Get home early tomorrow. No later than earlier."

After picking, poking, and tickling me, I jokingly told Joe to knock it off or I would punch his lights out. He responded: "Bring it on. Fight like a lady, I dare you!"

Joe (angrily): "I listen to my radio. I not watch *World's Dumbest Videos.*"
Me: "What did you want to watch?"
Joe (like I'm an idiot): "*South Beach Towing* or *Lizard Lick Towing.*"
Wow, hard to believe those two aren't the dumbest shows!

Joe does not work on Fridays, so it allows me to go to work very early those days. He stays home while Paul sleeps from his overnight shift. Notorious for getting into things during the time he is on his own, we tend to give him small jobs or a letter to write to keep him occupied. When Paul woke up one Friday, he heard an unfamiliar water sound. He sneaked down the hall to see what Joe was doing. He was in the bathroom (always with the door open), on his knees by the toilet. Paul thought, "Oh good, he's cleaning the toilet." No, no, he wasn't. Joe was swishing his eyeglasses through the toilet water really fast. He would hold them up to look at them to see if they were clean, and swish some more.

Startled by Paul's presence, he swished the glasses through the toilet water one more time and put them on his face, water running down his cheeks.

Paul asked, "WHAT are you doing, and please, tell me that water is clean?"

Joe proudly declared, "I cleaning them!"

Me: "I love you, Joe. Say your prayers."
Joe: "I don't like say prayers. They make me drowsy. Maybe some other time."

It's two degrees outside and feels cool in the house. Joe had taken a shower twenty minutes earlier and was still naked. Here is a sentence I never thought I would have to say: "Just get dressed Joe, it's too cold to be naked."

Joe, when I told him he might have to wear boots tomorrow: "I NOT like snow. Don't make me mad. I like spring."
Me: "I don't make the snow. God makes the snow."
Joe: "Well, tell God no more snow."
Me: "Sure Joe, I'll get right on it...sigh!"

Joe to Paul: "Will you stop laughing. I am serious, you know."
Paul: "I'm not laughing at you, I'm laughing with you."
Joe (sternly): "I am not laughing. I'm serious, NOT."

At a store checkout counter Joe announced, "Hey Paul, I found a girlfriend for you."

Paul responded, "Oh great, I'm sure my wife is happy to hear that."

Then Joe turned to the woman who was ringing up our purchases and said, "You can still have him if you want." She and the other women at the counter were still laughing as we left.

It was going to be one of those days: At 10 a.m. I told Joe no breakfast until he was dressed for the day. He refused, sort of. He came out with his pajamas on over his clothes. Oh, he was going to show me who's boss! All I could do was laugh and think, "Yes, you are my 44-year-old preschooler."

Joe seemed to have discovered the word "loser" overnight. As I tied his shoes in the morning before he went to work, he blurted out, "If you loser you not winner. If you win you are a winner, not a loser. If you a loser, you scrub floors." It was as if he had been fighting the devil on his shoulder all night trying to keep himself out of trouble, so he wouldn't have to clean the floors. And it worked, he behaved so he did not have to clean the floors.

I took Joe with me to Trader Joe's. He was fascinated with a young woman employee with very bright blue hair. To her, and my embarrassment, he loudly shouted from across the store: "Hey Sis, come here and look-it! She has BLUE HAIR." I walked over to claim him and to apologize to her. All was fine as he hugged it out with her, told her how much he liked her BLUE hair, and that she was beautiful. Her coworkers couldn't stop laughing.

As I handed Joe his fruit smoothie, I dropped it, spilling it all over the kitchen center island, and I said, "SUGAR."

Joe scolded, "WHAT? You don't say SUGAR! You say swear word like, 'OH SH@#.' Get it right next time. You get your words mixed up."

As I started down the street I looked back and saw Joe standing in his bedroom window with both arms and hands up with what I thought were both middle fingers extended. I went back up the driveway, into the house, and nose to nose with him. I said, "I am not putting up with any of that kind of nonsense today with you standing in the window giving me the middle finger on both hands."

Like I'm a real idiot he said, "I not give you two middle fingers. I ONLY give you one middle finger."

Poor Joe. Telling the truth is so painful:
>
> Were you ready for your driver this morning? "Yes."
> Were you ready for your driver this morning? "Maybe."
> Were you ready for your driver this morning? "No."
> Did you turn on my windshield wipers? "NOT ME."
> Did you turn on my windshield wipers? "Your brother did."

Harsh wake-up call. Last night, I promised Joe I'd turn the calendar to July before I went to bed, but I forgot. Then I overslept by an hour, which rarely happens. I woke up to: "Sister, get outta bed. Quit being so G** D*** lazy and get outta bed and change the calendar." Calendar has been changed and I'm up and at 'em now. I want to know who has been talking like that around him because Paul and I don't talk like that. Wow, good morning July!

After I tied Joe's shoes one morning, I kissed each of his cheeks and said, "I love you and now I am going in to take a shower."

In a vile tone of voice, he said, "You DISGUST me." Then he said he didn't want me to take a shower. He wanted me to "just rinse your hair in the kitchen sink."

Later in the day I was telling this to another sister and she said, "Don't feel bad. He's repeating lines from a commercial for cockroaches. Roaches take over the guy's house and are in the bathroom using the shower." I so wish I could get inside my brother's head and see and hear the world in which he lives.

Joe and I were running late in getting ready for work. As I was rushing Joe to get ready faster, he said, "You 'noxious. Don't get me dead going. Do I look like I in heaven? No. Mom and Dad in heaven. I HERE, getting ready." I think that was his way of telling me to back off, that he wasn't just laying around, rather, that he was getting ready as fast as he could.

Joe: "Hey Skinny Mini."
Me: "Me? I'm not a skinny mini."
Joe: "I know you aren't. Just kidding with you."

We reluctantly change the batteries in Joe's flashlight. In doing so we understand he will forego sleep to roam the house to "investigate," shine it out the windows in the wee hours, traipse through the neighborhood at 6 a.m., or use it to light the room so he can write his numbers in the darkest hours of the day. He might look like a raccoon from lack of sleep, but he is so delightfully happy when he gets the new batteries so his flashlight is working again.

I asked Joe what he would like for his birthday and Christmas. He said, "Batteries for my TV remote." When I told him I had just changed those batteries the week before he said, "That TV is not no good. I need a new one." The following week I asked him the same question and he said, "Roller blades." I guess a new TV isn't such a bad idea if I must choose between the two.

Throughout the year he'll randomly mention to me what he wants for his birthday or Christmas. His list is always interesting: a loaf of white bread, a case of a particular brand of soda, a new car, a new overhead garage door, a certain kind of candy bar, donuts, or even a cheeseburger.

"What are you doing?" I snarled at the truck that crossed into my lane.
Joe: "You swear."
"What? I did not swear."
Joe: "You need to swear. It is good for your heart."

It was the night before Joe's birthday. We were talking about him being 46 years old. He said, "I not old. You old if you ugly. I young, not old. I am not ugly." So, then Paul asked him if Paul's mother was old, Joe responded, "NOOO, she young. She is 94 years young."

Joe, shall we say, released some gas at dinner. That led to a short conversation about good table manners. I am not sure how Paul and I kept a straight face when Joe said, "Well, you can take me to the gas station and fill my bottom up with gas if you want to."

Having no concept of money, Joe told me, "Go buy some money for your brother, I need money."

Joe confessed that while I was gone he was swearing at me. He then asked, "What happens when you swear?"
In turn, I said, "You tell me. What happens when you swear?"
He thought for a second and said, "You go to prison, I think, or the Catholic church."

Chapter 7
MIXED-UP WORDS AND SENTENCES

Joe's simple, innocent and happy ways so touch my heart, and so do many of his comments, mixed-up words, and sentences.

Joe's mispronunciations of:
Hawaii – why-he
Lasagna – lllasagna
Salami – salllami
Teriyaki – takiyaki
Idiot – yidiot
Enchiladas – chilaaadas
Dramatic – traumatic
Christmas – ssscrismmas
Heimlich maneuver – heinny mover
Tetrazzini – takizini or takiakizini
Since – simps
Sunglasses – sun tennies
Humongous – hunkamunka
Que Pasa – kay pasta

Cabo San Lucas – Cabo San Kalucas
Amigos – comigos
"Well excuse me, duh, for nothing."
"Yeah, sure, right."
"My A."

Instead of "What's your point?" Joe says, "I've got the sign of the point."

Instead of the weather being "hot and muggy," Joe says, "hot and monkey."

Instead of "Excuse me for living," Joe says, "Well, excuse me for livid."

"I NOT your honey. I am your brother."

Regarding whatever meal has been prepared, "You are a specialist!"

"Seriously? Be honestly."

Instead of "Don't dish it out if you can't take it," Joe says, "Don't flush it out if you can't take it."

I came in from my walk. Joe greeted me at the garage door. He was in the middle of putting on his pajama top. It was on in a way that only his face was through, stopping at his hairline. I said, "Well, hello, Sister Mary Joe!"
"I nooooot Sister Mary Joe."
"Really? I thought you were Sister Mary Joe. You look like Sister Mary Joe."
"I Joe Burns, your brother!"

"You are the one great, brave sister that I have never met."

He had a cold and was coughing really bad. Once he stopped coughing, he said, "Ugh, I need mouth-to-mouth affection."

Joe and I were shoveling mulch for the gardens. Joe said, "Oh, my leg hurts. I need some Pepto-Bismol."
I didn't have the heart to tell him that Pepto-Bismol has nothing to do with sore legs.

Joe had just finished cleaning his glasses, and on the way to bed he said to me as he pointed to his eyeglasses, "Well, Spickel Span."
He meant the household cleaning product, Spic and Span, whose television commercials ended with, "It's not clean until it's Spic and Span!"

I asked, "Joe, what time is it? Can you look at the clock and tell me?"
With a deep sigh he reported the time, "It is quarter after nine after two." It was actually 9:30 p.m.

Joe asked me, "Want me to yell at you at the top of my ears?"

To his niece, "You are a stubborn mule. That means you are fat like a buffalo."

A neighbor had set off a firecracker outside. Joe asked, "What was that gunshot all about? It scared the wits out of my pants."

We were packing to move to a new house and Joe was helping. His knees cracked as he sat on the dining room floor to help with a box. He said, "Aaahh, I cracked my knee knuckles. That kind of hurts."

Goofing around and poking each other, I poked Joe on his chest. He said, "Don't poke me in my heartbeat."

When asked to take a shower, he replied, "Yes, I know. You tell me fifteen eighty-three times."

Joe set his shirt on the kitchen center island. He showed me the shirt and pointed to the word "Nike" on the front. He said, "See, Nike (pronounced to sound like bike)."

"No, it's Nik-eeee."

"Nooooooo, it say Nike."

"Well, not really Joe, they pronounce it Nik-eeeee."

"Nooooooo, it say Nike, like bike, hike, mike, not say Nik-eeeee (really sassy)."

"Ok, Joe, no more arguing from me. Nike it is."

"Seeeee, I tellllllll you thaaaaaaat!" (like I'm an idiot!)

"Hey Sis, I hear a parakeet outside."

"You do? You hear a parakeet? What does it sound like?"

"Yes. I hear a parakeet. It goes like this: (and he made a chirping sound)."

I looked and listened out his bedroom window. I said, "Are you sure it wasn't a cricket?"

"YES! It is a cricket, not a parakeet! I get my words mixed up. Blahhh! It is a cricket, not a parakeet!"

Joe: "We have French toast tomorrow."
Me: "No, I don't think we will have French toast this weekend."
Joe: "We have pancakes."
Me: "No, I don't think so."
Joe: "Yes, you can. Use your Monterey Jack."
He meant Hungry Jack pancake mix.

When Joe gave me a hug goodnight my nose was cold.
Joe: "Your nose is toasty cold."

"Hey Sis, look-it," Joe said, holding out his hand. "I have three cactuses. I find them on my shoestrings."

I said, "Oh, those are sandburs."

To which he replied, "I telllll you that!"

As Joe was heading to bed, I heard him messing with the dining room blinds, which he is not supposed to be touching. He said, "Your blinds are tingling."

"My what?"

"Your blinds are tickling on top."

What he meant was, the strings/cords of the window blinds were tangled, which bothers Joe to no end.

Joe dropped a container on the floor. "I have butterfingers."

I asked, "What?" Because I had been hungry for a Butterfinger all day!

He said, "I have butterfingers. I drop it. It fall out of my hand. Do you have Poly Grip?" (Poly Grip is for dentures.)

Joe: "I get bit by Skittles by my armpit."
Me: "Do you mean a skeeter, like a mosquito?"
Joe: "Yes, skeeters!"

Joe spent the weekend with our sister and her family. Our sister and her daughter were saying goodnight to Joe:
Sister: "I love you."
Joe: "I love you."
Niece: "I love you more!"
Joe: "I love you less!"

Joe, giving me a hug: "Come on…be my sugar plump!"

Instead of the common phrase 'Sweet Cheeks', Joe said to me: "Thanks, Sweet Cheese!"

"Oops, the downstairs clock didn't get changed for daylight saving time."
Joe: "It only 7:45. It NOT bedtime yet. Use your glasses to think!"

Me: "What did you make in cooking class today?"
Joe: "Spaghetti kiwi."
Me: "What did you make?"
Joe: "A big lemon; spaghetti kiwi."
Me: "Do you mean Spaghetti Squash?"
Joe: "YES! I tell you that!"

Joe: "I give you kisses on this cheek and one on this cheek, and one on your 'bald.'"
Me: "Do you mean my forehead?"
Joe: "Yes! Your forehead."

I checked in on Joe to be certain he wasn't napping. It was debatable, but he said, "I not sleeping. My eyes is wide closed."

Joe: "You look like a tidal wave."
Me: "A tidal wave?"
Joe: "Oh, no. You look like a tub of lard."
Me: "Well, that's not a kind thing to say."
Joe: "Look! You look fat like me. See my fat tummy? You look fat like this."

"Joe, do you want cheese on your burger?"
"Yes, I have vanilla cheese." He meant Velveeta cheese.

Chapter 8

TELEPHONE JOE

Joe was in his early twenties and still living with our parents. While Mom and Dad were downstairs, Joe went upstairs in one of the bedrooms that had a telephone. He knew my sister's long-distance telephone number by heart and he dialed it. He dialed it, and dialed it, and dialed it—243 times. Frustrated that the answering machine picked up each time he called, Joe would listen to the message, hang up, and dial again. Imagine my parent's surprise when their telephone bill arrived with all those charges on it.

Joe has had a lifelong fascination with the telephone, but mainly the telephone book. If ever the phone book was not where it should be, we knew where to look. Joe would have a stack of phone books from years past, generally opened to the yellow pages, stacked on the desk in his bedroom. He would go page by page, counting each page. Then, he would look through the yellow pages, eventually landing on his other fascination, the overhead garage door section.

It was all very benign until he repeatedly dialed the number of a random business listed in the yellow pages. On a Friday morning, Paul and Joe had just pulled into the garage with a van full of groceries. Paul sensed someone was behind him in the driveway and he looked in the rearview mirror to find a police officer parked behind the van. Before getting out of the van, Paul asked Joe, "What did you do?" Then, Joe saw the officer and became scared, so he would not get out of the van right away. The officer told Paul that for weeks Joe had been calling the number of the business and that the calls were coming from our home phone. Because the calls were placed before business hours, the answering machine would pick up. Generally, Joe would just take a deep breath and leave a big sigh into the phone, or he would grumble about them not being open. But, on this day, upset because the answering machine picked up again, Joe threatened "I kill you." Joe's eyes were as big as saucers. Paul told the police officer, "Take him away!" Of course, Paul was kidding. The officer said, "Not this time I won't but we will have to think about it the next time." She also told Paul that the business blocked our phone number, so it shouldn't be a problem again.

After putting the groceries away, Paul called me at work and told me about what had happened. I called the business from my work phone and explained to the manager who Joe was, that we were unaware he had been placing the phone calls to them, and that we sincerely apologize for the threatening nature of his phone message. She was very gracious and appreciated the apology, yet, understandably, she still sounded a bit rattled by the message.

That was not my first time having to call someone to apologize for Joe's repeated phone calling. Years earlier Joe would dial the number of our childhood phone. When our family home was sold, and Joe came to live with me and my family, the old phone number was given to another customer. Periodically, I would catch Joe just hanging up the phone, or attempting to dial a number. Finally, I caught him in the act and talking to a person. Turning the phone over to me, I explained to the young woman that my brother Joe has Down syndrome and that her telephone number was once our family's phone number for many, many years. Fortunately, Joe had not said anything threatening or inappropriate, and she, too, appreciated my apology and promise that he would not call her again. A promise, I believe, which he has kept to this day.

Telephone Joe

The funniest and most embarrassing phone call Joe has made was the one when he called my work. A vice president, who had the same last four digits in his work phone number, but in a different order than mine, received a voice mail message. Unable to fully understand what the caller was saying, he asked one of the women in his office to come and listen to the message. She also had difficulty understanding some of the words. Then, another office member was invited in to hear the message. She exclaimed, "Sandra! That message is for Sandra! That is her brother." So, they forwarded the message to me. The message was, "Sandra is a F***erFace."

Chapter 9
MISBEHAVING JOE

Often when Joe has exceptionally sassy or unpredictable behavior, we will have him scrub a sink or toilet, or we'll give him a cloth to wipe down the floors. He doesn't like to do the floors because it hurts his knees. However, for the few minutes he is on a kneeling pad on the floor, his behavior improves so it is an effective solution.

Early one morning I had spilled water on the kitchen rug, so I hung it up to dry. When I got home from work, I was in another room of the house when I heard Paul ask how the rug got all wet. I called out that I had done it. In the meantime, Joe was defending himself, "I not do it. I NOT spill water on the rug. Not me."

I called out again that I had spilled a glass of water on the floor.

A moment later Joe stormed into the room with arms crossed and scolded me: "That is inexcusable, unacceptable, uncalled for, and unbelievable. You need consequences. You need to scrub floor with sore knees."

Joe, age thirty-five, was staying at our sister's home for the weekend. They live out in the country and have a lot of things in their garage that we don't, such as farming equipment and tools, axes and other things for chopping wood for their wood burner stove, etc. Their only neighbors, who Joe knows very well, live about 30–40 yards away. Very early one summer morning, still quite dark outside, Joe snuck out of the house, and knocked on their front door. The neighbor opened the door and asked if our sister knew he was over at his house. Joe gave his standard response, "I dunno." They then sent him back to our sister's house. A short time later, Joe again returned to the neighbor's house with an axe he found in our sister's garage. He went up to the house, looked in, and shattered their window with the axe. The neighbors ran downstairs to find Joe by the front door with the axe in his hands. He just wanted to say hello.

After dinner I asked Joe to scrub his toilet while Paul and I took a walk. He was so offended, "I NOT swear! I not be naughty. I NOT clean bathroom." I had to tell him that Paul has to clean the basement bathroom, and that I have to clean our bedroom bathroom, so he has to clean his bathroom. "Hmmmmmppp!" was all I heard. When we got home from our walk he was sitting on the floor, legs wrapped around the toilet bowl, nearly scrubbing the white off the bowl. It was such a cute, yet icky sight, with his face right down by the toilet seat.

At supper Paul said he would need Joe's help the next morning by taking the rugs outside and shaking them. Paul's request must have taken a few minutes to sink in. Joe began carrying on a conversation with both himself and to me about not liking the fact that he would have to shake rugs the next morning. His mumbling went on for several minutes and included something about scrubbing sinks.

I finally realized what he was chattering about. When Paul came back in the room I told Joe to tell Paul what he was saying.

Joe clearly, as clearly as Joe could, told Paul that he did NOT want to shake the rugs, saying, "How about you shake rugs, I scrub the kitchen sink, my bathroom sink and tub. I not shake rugs." I loved his negotiation skills, and Paul agreed to the deal.

My day started at 4:30 a.m. with me scolding Joe, telling him to get back in bed, that it is too early to be up. It ended with more reprimanding. When I asked him to wash his hands after toileting, he responded, "Why don't you spell 'drop dead.'"

I was giving Joe instructions for the next morning and said, "No spitting and no bad words."
Joe: "You mean like the B word?"
"Beautiful?"
Joe: "No, you a B-I-T-C-H!"

While in the lunchroom at his work, Joe was mad that he had a container of yogurt in his lunchbox. He took the yogurt cup in both hands, top still sealed. He squeezed it with two hands with all his might until the yogurt squirted out all over the wall, table, and floor. Then he refused to clean up the mess. Once home, he had no choice but to write an apology letter to the lunch ladies.

Sly Joe unlocked the front door before he left for work. I noticed it and relocked it. As I talked with him about it, and knowing he was lying, I asked, "Well, if you didn't do it, who did?"
He said, "The wind."
I replied, "Joe, I know you are not being honest or telling me the truth."
With a sass in his voice he said, "Well, Jimmy Crack Corn, and really, I don't care, Sister."
End of conversation. I couldn't let him see me laughing.

Some people write love notes...some brothers write anger notes. He was upset because I told him I would not be home until after 4 p.m. that day. He wants me home at 3 p.m. I found a handwritten note in my work bag as I put my lunch in, which said, "F***er O'Clock." Guess who did not get dessert that night?

Chapter 10

INSPIRATIONAL JOE

For all of Joe's naughtiness, swearing, and cunning behavior, he has also been an inspiration to others, particularly, to a couple of his nieces and nephews.

Joe was a very tiny infant when I began to beg my mom, asking if she would bring baby Joey to one of my Girl Scout meetings. Eventually, she brought him to the school where we met and showed the girls some of the characteristics of a person with Down syndrome and explained how he was different than us. I was so excited to finally be able to show him off to the girls in my troop.

So, it was no surprise to me when our daughter Beth asked if she could take Joe to her middle school health class and "show and tell" Joe, just as my mom had with me and the Girl Scouts. Joe, in his mid-twenties, loved it. He loved all the attention, especially when he would say or do something funny to make Beth's classmates laugh.

One sister would frequently bring Joe to our niece's middle and high school to eat lunch with her and her classmates. The students all loved it. Joe may have unwittingly changed the perception of some who may have thought people with disabilities are scary or strange, or any number of other things. Many times, people become nervous or uncertain around someone who is not like themselves. My niece simply wanted to have Joe join her for lunch because she loves him so, and she knew how funny he could be, and he usually proved her right. Joe would be silly, funny, and loveable with my niece and her friends.

Now in college, my niece's classmates and friends still ask her about Uncle Joe. In fact, we recently were at the mall shopping. One of her friends said hello to Joe as we walked by. He, remembering her name, said hello and gave her a big hug.

In one of my niece's college courses, she had to give a speech on the local nonprofit organization where Joe has worked for 26 years. She interviewed Joe and me, asking lots of questions about individuals with Down syndrome, about Joe in particular, his jobs, and other assorted facts and stories. She knew her subject so well, she received the highest score of all the speeches her classmates presented.

A nephew wrote a high school paper his senior year of high school about Uncle Joe being a role model to him, without Joe even knowing it. He cited Joe's organization, "how Joe has a precise spot for everything in his room and if out of place, he instantly returns the item to where it should be." He wrote about how Joe follows a very particular routine, when he gets up, when he goes to bed, and each of the tasks he does in between throughout the day, and in a very certain order. His nephew shared how Joe is very patient, he doesn't complain if he is bored or if someone is taking too long.

My favorite part of our nephew's school paper about Joe is when he wrote: "There is not a time where people are around Uncle Joe and haven't laughed or at least cracked a smile, no matter the mood. By just the way his personality is, it is hard not to like him. Joe is that loving kind of guy that will give anyone a hug and who has a compliment for everyone. If you talk to Joe long enough you will notice he has his little sayings like, 'I do fine,' when asked how he is, or always answering yes or no questions with a Spanish 'si.' Not only does Joe have a comical way of talking at times, his laugh and facial expressions are just as interesting. If he is ever asked something that is baffling or unexpected, he has a nice way of expressing a response with his body language. Along with his actions, responses, and body language, his other way of lightening the mood is when he gets laughing at something funny. It is a guarantee that his hysterical laugh is going to be more comical than the punch line. When in doubt, or having a lousy day, just go have a conversation with my Uncle Joe."

Beth has also written a college paper about her Uncle Joe. She wrote of how he has influenced her in so many ways, and as a result has made her a better person. He has taught her to grow and to be her own person; he has taught her to look at every person with an open heart.

Beth was twelve years old when Joe came to live with our family. Beth explained that Joe living with us was one of the best things in her life: how he taught her patience, humor, love, how to give and how to care for others, how to be optimistic when there is tension in the air, and how to offer a helping hand when there are those in need.

Uncle Joe made such an impact on Beth that she felt it was necessary to give back to him and others with varying abilities. She majored in and works in a field where she not only helps children and adults with Down syndrome, but also those with a wide variety of disabilities.

I loved that Beth wrote: "Joe's heart is filled with nothing but love. If there is one thing he has taught me that I feel I can share and pass on to other people, it is to look at every person with an open heart, no matter what the extent of their ability or disability. Many people go through life without ever interacting with someone with a disability. Many of those who do, are uncertain of how they will act around such a person, and therefore, they tend to act odd themselves. If you have the opportunity to interact or be around someone who has a disability, cherish the time you have with that person, because you can learn so much from them about life and love."

At Beth and Brian's wedding ceremony, her father Paul walked her halfway down the aisle to where Joe was standing, all spiffy in his suit pants, vest, and tie, looking very dapper. Joe proudly looped his arm

Paul and Joe walking Beth down the aisle.

around Beth's free arm and together Paul and Joe walked Beth the rest of the way down the aisle. Paul, bless his heart, knew how important this special moment was to Beth. Having both her dad and Joe walk her down the aisle at her wedding was something she had long talked about since she was in high school.

Two weeks before their wedding, the person officiating asked Paul and me for a sentence or two of wedding advice, serious or funny, for Beth and Brian.

A couple of days later at dinner, Paul and I discussed this request and came up with very practical, sturdy parental words of advice. Meaning to be funny, I then turned to Joe and asked him if he had any wedding advice for Beth and Brian. Without any coaxing he immediately said:

"Beth, give him treats (like ice cream sandwiches), and hugs and kisses. Brian, give Beth lots of kisses and go out on lunch dates."

Without telling anyone else, other than the officiant, whom we sworn to secrecy, Uncle Joe's exact quote was read into the ceremony along with the wise advice of Paul and me, as well as Brian's parents and grandparents. It melted my heart and the hearts of many in attendance. It was such a treasured moment.

Further, when Beth and Brian's first child was born, he was given the middle name of Joseph, after Uncle Joe. Joe proudly tells people, "He named after me. I his Uncle Joe."

Joe and Sandra at Beth's wedding.

Two years later, our son Bryan became engaged to Kristy. Every time wedding planning conversations came up, Joe would tell us, "I walk Kristy down the aisle." It took a long time to convince him otherwise, that Kristy's dad would get to do that. So, at the civil ceremony preformed a week before their destination wedding out of the country, when Bryan asked Joe to be the ring bearer, Joe was thrilled. He took his responsibility very seriously. He listened intently for when the chaplain asked for the rings, at which time he proudly walked up and handed the ring box to the chaplain. He came back to where the parents and other family were seated, the only guests there, and with a big, broad smile, he gave Paul and me the thumbs up. He was so proud of himself.

Since Joe's marriage advice for Beth and Brian was such a hit, I decide to ask Joe what advice he had to give to Bryan and Kristy. Without anyone knowing, including Paul, each night for two weeks prior to Bryan and Kristy's official wedding ceremony, I had Joe practice reading the toast he was going to give to the newlyweds at the reception. I wanted him to be very comfortable, clear, loud, and prepared to read it when the time came. I would mute the television and tell him to read it real loud, "so all the people on the television can hear you." I gave him a wooden spoon or a hair brush to hold, pretending it was a microphone. Satisfied, I crossed my fingers and prayed he would perform spot-on perfect.

When we got to the reception area, without even asking, I told the gentleman in charge of the venue that after the best man and matron of honor gave their toasts to Bryan and Kristy that Joe would also be giving a toast; however, he was not to tell anyone. No one. Joe and I had practiced reading the toast again three different times earlier in the day. Finally, the big moment came. The best man gave his toast. As he was preparing to turn the microphone over to the matron of honor, surprisingly, Joe stood up, intercepted the microphone, and with everyone quietly listening, he read his toast beautifully, to much applause and laughter. He read the toast that he had so diligently practiced:

"May your marriage be happy and healthy,
with lots of kisses and kids, laughter and love.
Bryan, you can kiss Kristy now.
If you don't, I will!"

Chapter 11
PECULIAR JOE

Like many things with Joe, there is not a lot of "in between." He is either meticulously precise, or quite the opposite, messy and dirty. He has a peculiar way about him in that he will perfectly align the plates in the dishwasher so the manufacturer's label on the backside is in a certain direction, he will arrange the placemats, napkins, and silverware just so on the table, and he will align the rugs evenly with the lines of the wood floors, and of course, all the light switches must be in the "correct" direction in which he approves. He can't sleep if the blinds are not positioned at the perfect angle or if the cords are twisted.

Towels and clothing are neatly folded, as are the tissues before he uses them to blow his nose; even his dirty socks are neatly stacked in the dirty laundry basket. One can bounce a quarter on his bed it's so perfectly made.

On the other hand, Joe thinks nothing of sneezing or coughing (after just having had cherry cough medicine, mind you) or spitting all over the blinds, walls, windows, or floors. One nasty habit we quickly nipped in the bud upon the move to our new home was his spitting over the stairway to the basement while brushing his teeth when we are not around to see him do it. He often touches the walls or doorways with his hands, both clean or dirty hands, so they get scrubbed on a frequent basis, as does the carpet.

Joe is oh, so wasteful and hard on things. We have automatic liquid soap dispensers at every sink, so it is easier to use and more sanitary, eliminating having to touch a soap bar or pump bottle. Unfortunately, he manipulates the amount of soap that comes out for each use. The palm of his hand will overflow with soap, and then he will run the water until every soap bubble is down the drain. We buy him the cheapest shampoo on the market because he uses an excessive amount of it with each shower. He is very good about brushing his teeth but the amount he uses is about an inch thick piled high on the brush. He also uses an inordinate amount of toilet paper.

Currently, the house rule is that Joe cannot touch the blinds in his bedroom because in the eight years we have lived in our home, we have replaced the custom-ordered blinds three times due to his destructive nature when opening or closing them.

Joe is also very peculiar when using the bathroom, and he certainly does not understand the word privacy. He closes and locks the bathroom door when he showers but will open the door as soon as he is out of the shower and still naked. His bedroom and bathroom are near the front of the house so if someone comes to the door, they could be in for quite a sight with Joe naked and not in any hurry to get dressed. It makes no difference to Joe if the blinds in his bedroom are open, and he will walk naked right up to the window to see what is happening outside.

On a late summer afternoon, Paul and I were running an errand and gone for only an hour. Joe was instructed to put on his pajamas and to brush his teeth while we were gone. A few days later the neighbor told us that while he was mowing the lawn he looked up and saw Joe. Joe must have heard the mower and went outside to say hello to the neighbor. Naked.

Peculiar Joe

Not a care in the world and without a stitch of clothing. The neighbor encouraged Joe to go inside and put on his pajamas before we came home.

Joe is fascinated by overhead garage doors and the number of windows in a garage door, as well as the big green electrical boxes on the front lawns of some neighborhoods. I can't explain either, other than it is just Joe's "thing" and he will take every opportunity he can to count all the garage door windows as he takes a walk. In the car he will often point out garage doors and tell us the number of windows.

Joe loves calendars. He will, what we call, study the calendar. He spends many hours reading the calendar, discussing what is on the calendar that Paul or I have penciled in. Because of this, he also knows who has a birthday, how old they will be and on what day and date. In fact, he knows how old and what day family member's birthdays are for the next few years.

A man with very distinctive handwriting, Joe will write, and write, and write some more. What he writes changes from time to time, but he will

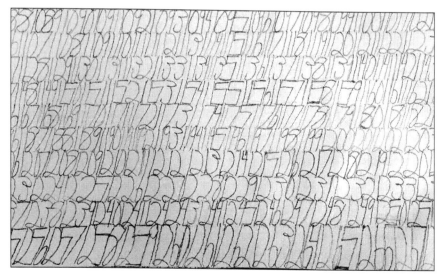

Joe's number writing in his distinctive handwriting style.

write the same thing for months on end. For several months he would write the numbers one through seven. When I asked him why he only writes one through seven he said in a matter-of-fact manner, "Because there are only seven days (in a week)." Growing up he had stacks of papers in which he wrote numbers beginning with one up through several thousands. Now he typically writes on three-inch by three-inch paper squares, which he keeps neatly stacked in his desk drawer. These days his fascination is with writing all the songs from one of his favorite Barry Manilow CDs. He will write these over and over for hours and hours. He has been known to get up in the wee hours of the morning, go into his bathroom, cover the counter with his squares of papers, kneel on the floor, and write until it is time to get up and ready for work. It usually results in a very crabby Joe for the rest of the day.

Of course, each of us has our own set of peculiarities, those are a few of Joe's. Some are annoying or expensive, others are harmless.

The Clean Underwear Caper
Paul called me at work, "Joe's up to his old tricks again." He was referring to Joe not changing his underwear for days at a time. Days earlier I had told him to put all his laundry in the hamper in his bedroom. He had been tossing it into the laundry basket on top of the dryer. My concern was him overshooting the basket and clothes being tossed behind the dryer. The next night, a Sunday, standing naked, Joe tossed his underwear into the basket atop the dryer. He refused to take them out and put them in his hamper. I took the dirty underwear from the laundry room and dramatically put them into his hamper. Joe was not happy. He grabbed them out of the hamper and angrily slammed them onto his bed. I ignored his actions, didn't say a word and left his bedroom.

Tuesday, before supper I checked his hamper and saw no white laundry. I found them on the chair next to his dresser. I called him to his room, asking, "What are these?"

He said, "My dirty clothes."

I told him, "Well, there is your hamper. Please put them in the hamper."

He said, "Noooo way."

To which I calmly responded, "That's fine. You don't need to. You simply won't eat supper tonight until they are in the hamper," and walked out of the room. Whoosh! In the hamper they went and quickly at the dinner table he sat.

Wednesday, after work I looked in his hamper to check again; nope, no white laundry. Prior to his bedtime, I checked Joe's hamper again; no whites. Obviously, he ate dinner last night and promptly removed them from the hamper. After a look around his bedroom, I found his pile of whites "hiding" under his chair. As Joe said goodnight to me I calmly said, "I hope you have been putting your underwear and all of your other dirty clothes into the hamper in your bedroom."

He just looked at me with a funny look, not sure of what to say, and giving up the good fight, said, "I see you in the morning. Good night," and walked to his bedroom.

Chapter 12

TELL IT LIKE IT IS, JOE

Joe has always gotten along with Paul and appreciates what Paul does for him. But honestly, many days Joe would be really happy if Paul had to work seven days a week, just so he would be gone, and Joe could have me all to himself.

One evening before Paul went to work, Joe picked up Paul's wallet and car keys. He said to me, "His wallet and keys are cold." I asked what Paul should do to warm them up. He responded: "Put his wallet in his pocket, put his key in the van, and get him gone."

I was standing on the kitchen counter doing spring house cleaning above the cabinets. As I was stepping down onto a chair, I told Joe, "Do not touch my bottom."

His response, "That is no bottom. That is a big fat BUTT."
Honest Joe—1; Humbled Sandra—0

Joe went downstairs to see what was on television. He came back upstairs sounding upset and said: *Everybody Loves Raymond*. I don't." And off to his bedroom and radio he went!

He tattled on himself for calling two people at work "fatso."

When asked if they were heavy he said, "Yes, they are chunky! I not lying."

I asked if he was chunky. "Noooo, I slim."

I love how honest, yet how clueless, he is.

As we left the grocery store I was scolding Joe for hugging and kissing the teen-aged checkout girl.

Me: "Any other 44-year-old man would be in jail for kissing and hugging a teenager like that. You cannot be kissing people like that. It is inappropriate behavior."

Joe: "Oh Sister, no it is not. Kissing is good for you, you know. I am a woman lover!"

I was home sick from work. Joe came home from his job, looked at me, and said: "You look like a dump."

Me: "Do you mean I look down in the dumps?"

Joe: "Yes, I tell you that. You look dumpy!"

I'm feeling better already, thanks Joe!

Best scolding ever from Joe, and so true:

"You are the biggest problem with your mouth. I don't like your shouting. I am not laughing, I am serious."

As he was getting into the back seat of the car he said, "Ouch!" Bryan asked, "Did you pull your groin?"

Joe said, "No, my testicles."

Joe was telling me about the woman who drives him home from work on Wednesdays. "She wear makeup; she has yellow teeth."

When I asked what color my teeth are, he said "white."

Whew!

"Blind? I NOT blind. Those are blinds (pointing to the window blinds). Take my word for it. I am not that smart."

Joe gave me the finger on his way downstairs to watch television. I told him that was not nice. Ten minutes later he yelled up the stairs to me, "I'm just going to sit down here and think about it." I asked what he was going to think about. He said, "Why I am such a failure. I need to have nice words and nice fingers, oh man."

We all have our struggles in life!

Joe had a rough day. First, he lost having dessert for giving me the finger. Then, he had to sit in the backseat of the car that picks him up for work, for swearing. Finally, at lunch another participant took Joe's soda and drank it.

Joe confessed, "I punch him in the back and I say, 'Nice going you fat head moron crazy bastard.' Then I swear your name 46 times, Sandra is a F***erFace."

I somewhat jokingly asked, "But, how did you really feel?"

Joe went on to say, "I only flip him off one time and I tell him, 'I want to pick you up and shove you into the kitchen sink.'"

I think he probably slept quite well that night after getting all of that off his chest.

Joe looked out the window and saw that it was snowing and proclaimed, "God make me mad. I NOT like snow. I like summer. The weatherman is a crazy bastard."

Chapter 13

JOE'S JAUNTS

A neighbor told Paul that Joe had gone into their backyard, climbed over their three-foot fence, ran across the yard, climbed up and over their four-foot retaining wall and finally, up and over a small hill at 6:15 a.m. The neighbor said this was not the first time he had done that, so they thought they had better let us know.

When Joe was asked why he went through their yard, he said he didn't want to walk up the street and around. He preferred this shortcut to get to neighbors Neil and Cortney's house. He said, "I not too crazy about the two dogs who barked at me (as he went through their yard on the other side of the hill). I tell the dogs to shut up and stop your barking."

Before I left for work at 5:45 a.m. on a cold January morning, I told Joe that Paul was very sick, and that Joe needed to be really good and real quiet, so Paul could sleep.

I was less than a mile from work at 6:10 a.m. and Cortney, a nearby neighbor told me that Joe just did a ding-dong-dash. Mind you, a not-so-fast dash. Joe then came back a second time a few moments later. This time, instead of ringing the doorbell only once, he ding-ding-ding-ding-

dinged the doorbell repeatedly. When Cortney opened the door Joe said, "I say hello to you!" After she found out he was fine, that I was at work, and that Paul was sleeping, she scolded him for ringing the bell and for waking the kids and told him to go back home. He was in his pajamas, boots, and jacket, and carrying a flashlight.

He later told me, "I just say hi to Cortney My Love (as he calls her) and say happy birthday to Neil." Neil's birthday wasn't for several more weeks. Joe loves these two neighbors so much that I sometimes worry that we have a stalker on our hands.

There have been times when it seems Joe's only thoughts for weeks are of Cortney and Neil. One night he said to me, "When you die I go live with Cortney and Neil." On occasion I will request a "play date" with Neil and Joe where Joe will go over and sit in a chair and chat with Neil while he works on a project in his garage. That seems to satisfy Joe for a while, so he doesn't go over there as often.

Another day, Joe took a short walk to visit with Neil, but only if he was in his garage working. Neil wasn't home, and the garage door was closed. So, Joe looked in through the window of their front door, then another window, and next their children's bedroom windows. Cortney saw Joe but since he didn't ring the doorbell or knock on the door, she thought she would just observe him to see what he would do. Joe walked around to the back of the house. As he looked in the living room window, she went to find her phone to take a photo of him. He moved on to the patio door and looked in the house. Cortney took the picture of Peeping Joe, and then opened the door to chat with him for a few minutes before he went back to finish his walk.

When he got home he happily announced, "I home. I see Cortney and the kids!"

I asked several questions: "Was Neil home?"

"No."

"Was Cortney outside?"

"Nope."
"Did you ring the doorbell?"
Joe answered, "Nope."
"Did you knock on the door?"
"Nope. I look in all the windows. I go to back door. I see Cortney."

I asked, "Was Cortney dressed?"

"Yup! She wear pajama shirt and she wear pajama pants."

And then I called Cortney to apologize. She was amused by how accurately he explained it all, including the pajamas. We have since added a new rule to the "taking-a-walk" rule book: No looking in anyone's house windows!"

Joe peeping through the neighbor's window. Photo courtesy Cortney Molling

When Joe has a particularly sassy mouth or unruly behavior, we send him out on an "attitude adjustment walk." It truly does change his attitude, and he comes back home in a much better frame of mind. That was not the case one sunny summer day. As I laced up and tied his shoes, I told him I expected him to think about his behavior and swear words. He said, "Nope, I give you the finger." Without another word, I sent him outside. Watching him out the window, he headed up the street with his middle finger extended and arm raised up in the air. Our house is situated where we can see him walking around the block on three different sides of the block. He never lowered his arm or his finger the entire way around the block. Neighbors still talk about the day they saw him taking that walk.

It was a beautiful day and Joe went outside to take a walk. Paul asked him to stay on the sidewalks and out of the dirt as he walked through the neighborhood. Concrete contractors were in the process of pouring cement for the sidewalks in front of a home being built. Well, Joe stayed on the sidewalk. In fact, he stepped right into the freshly poured concrete. He took about six steps in it until it became too difficult to take another step forward. He stepped out of the cement and tried to shake it off. The concrete crew, who were now working on another section of sidewalk on the opposite side of the property, had not yet roped off the section where the concrete was just poured. Now realizing what had just happened, they ran over to help Joe. The attitude of the crew in wanting to help Joe was a real lesson in humanity. They were not angry at all. Instead, they took him over to where they had their equipment, helped him take off his shoes and socks, and hosed down his ankles and feet. They cleaned off his socks and shoes as best they could and sent him on his way. They then repaired the damaged sidewalk. When Joe came home, I noticed his wet socks and shoes and asked him what happened. He told me very clearly what happened, and then assured me that he did not swear at the cement or the workmen.

While I was out for an early morning walk, at 5:30 a.m., Joe was supposed to be getting dressed and ready for work. Instead, he went across the street to a neighbor's, while still in his jammies and slippers, to tell them their garage light was on. Fortunately, they were up and getting ready to leave for the airport, so he didn't wake them.

Joe was crabby, grumpy, sassy, and swearing when Paul told him to pick his own consequence, and that he would not get lunch until he did it. Eventually, on his own he went downstairs to clean the bathroom sink and toilet.

Joe ate lunch and to Paul's surprise, he then announced in a mad tone: "I go for walk," and out the door he went. He had been gone for more than 45 minutes when Paul went to check on Joe. Paul found him sitting on the sidewalk at the house next door to Neil and Cortney's. Apparently, he was waiting for Neil to get home.

The next day I got a Facebook message from another neighbor who lives near Neil and Cortney saying, "Where Paul found Joe yesterday, he had been there rolling around on the sidewalk for a good 45 minutes after checking out a few houses on our side of the street. I was out doing yard work so was keeping an eye on him. I had heard so many stories about Joe from other neighbors, it was good to put the face with the name."

Joe went out for a walk. He stopped at a home under construction. The builders were very concerned about Joe being so close to the construction site and worried he would hurt himself. Joe refused to leave when they asked him to, so they called the police to do a welfare check on Joe. The officer drove around the neighborhood, spotted Joe and stopped to talk to him. Joe told the officer he was okay, and where he lived. When the officer asked him other questions, Joe apparently did not want to answer them. Instead, he waved off the officer saying, "I am fine. You can leave now."

Then Joe started to walk back home, but not until he gave the officer the middle finger. At that point, Paul and I received a visit from the officer. In his own special way, Joe apologized to the policeman by reaching out to shake the officer's hand and saying, "Truce?" The officer, trying not to laugh, shook Joe's hand. Then Joe agreed he would never give the finger or swear at police officers, nor would he hang around construction sites.

Like my parents before us, Paul and I have been extremely fortunate to have such kind and caring neighbors in both neighborhoods where we have lived over the years Joe has been with us. All our neighbors have been very tolerant and very forgiving, especially those parents with young children who hear and see Joe's middle finger business and his swearing, as he takes a walk throughout the neighborhood. We are keenly aware that no other adult could get away with going outside naked, or looking in house windows, or coming right up into someone's garage uninvited, even if it is only to see what brand of overhead garage door they have. We are humbled by the neighbors who have shown their concern for Joe, his well-being and his safety—whether it be a phone call, text, or Facebook message to let us know where he is or what he is doing—such as sitting in the middle of the street for no good reason, for the past twenty minutes, or that he just went down the walking trail and they thought we should know. We are also very appreciative of our neighbors, parents and children alike, who stop to chat with Joe. It helps Joe to connect with others, to feel more independent, and it brings him much happiness. We know this, because he shares with us as soon as he comes home from his walk, the conversations he has with those who have taken a few moments out of their day to talk with him.

CLOSING COMMENTS

Individuals with Down syndrome have the power to make other people happy. There's no question that Joe has made people happy—with his smile, his words, his actions, and his love.

I cannot, not even for one second, imagine my life without Joe. He carries my heart in the palm of his hand, as I do his. My life changed exponentially, for the better, the moment Joe was born.

My marriage to Paul changed the moment Paul suggested we have Joe live with us on a permanent basis, after all, he had been living with us four days a week for the first three years after my mom's death, what was three more days? Suggesting we take Joe full time was a real testament to Paul's true character. I am fully aware it has not always

Joe in 2015, forty-five years old.

been easy to take a back seat to Joe, but Paul has selflessly done so time and time again.

The lives of Bryan and Beth changed profoundly when Uncle Joe moved in to our home. They were thirteen and twelve, very impressionable ages. Bryan gave up his bedroom for Joe. Both frequently babysat for Joe, giving us a much-needed break from the responsibility of the constant care and supervision Joe required. Because of Joe we did not take as many family vacations as we may have without him living with us. On the other hand, Joe taught Bryan and Beth so much about life, love, humor, and kindness at an age when children need it most, and something they have gracefully carried into their adult lives and marriages.

Joe is our forever child, given to us to raise, but to the world to love. With that, I leave you with this, one of my favorite conversations I have had with Joe:

"Joe, do you have Down syndrome?"

Joe: "No" (and he proceeds to name four co-worker friends who do).

"Do you have a disability?"

Joe: "Noooo. I am fine. I am perfect."

"Yes, you are. You are perfect just the way you are, aren't you?"

Joe: "Yup!"

Made in the USA
Lexington, KY
26 May 2018